SaaS

Everything you need to know about building successful Software as a Service Company in one place.

Table of Contents

Chapter 1: Introduction to SaaS

What is SaaS?

Software as a Service, or SaaS, represents a fundamental shift in the way software is delivered and consumed. In essence, SaaS is a cloud-based software distribution model that allows users to access and use applications over the internet, on a subscription basis, rather than installing and maintaining software on their local devices or servers. With SaaS, the software is hosted, managed, and updated by a third-party provider, freeing users from the hassles of installation and maintenance. This model is an innovative departure from traditional software deployment and has gained immense popularity in recent years.

The Evolution of Software Delivery Models

To truly appreciate the significance of SaaS, it's essential to understand how it fits into the broader landscape of software delivery models. Before SaaS became mainstream, software was typically distributed using two primary models: on-premises software and client-server applications.

On-premises software involved installing software directly on a user's device or within their organization's data center. Users were responsible for maintaining, updating, and troubleshooting the software. This model was prevalent for many years, but it came with several limitations, including high upfront costs, slow adoption of software updates, and the need for specialized IT staff to manage the infrastructure.

The client-server model, on the other hand, introduced a more distributed approach. In this model, applications were hosted on central servers and accessed by clients, usually over a network. While this approach improved software distribution, it still required significant infrastructure and maintenance efforts.

SaaS emerged as a response to the shortcomings of these earlier models. It provides a more flexible and cost-effective alternative to traditional software deployment. With SaaS, users can access software from any device with an internet connection, eliminating the need for extensive local infrastructure and reducing the burden of software maintenance.

Benefits and Challenges of SaaS

SaaS offers a host of advantages that have made it increasingly popular in the business world and among individual users.

Cost-Effective: One of the primary benefits of SaaS is its cost-effectiveness. Users no longer need to purchase expensive software licenses or invest in dedicated hardware. Instead, they pay for SaaS on a subscription basis, often with predictable monthly or annual fees.

Scalability: SaaS solutions are designed to scale with the needs of the user or organization. This scalability ensures that you can easily add or reduce resources as your requirements change.

Accessibility: SaaS applications are accessible from anywhere with an internet connection. This accessibility promotes collaboration, remote work, and flexibility, making it an attractive option for businesses and individuals alike.

Automatic Updates: SaaS providers handle software updates and maintenance, ensuring that users always have access to the latest features and security enhancements without manual interventions.

Reduced IT Overhead: SaaS eliminates the need for in-house IT staff to manage software and hardware, as most of the responsibility is shifted to the service provider.

Despite these benefits, SaaS is not without its challenges.

Data Security: Storing data off-site can raise concerns about data security and privacy. Users must trust SaaS providers to implement robust security measures to protect their information.

Internet Dependency: SaaS applications rely on an internet connection. If the connection is unreliable or goes down, users may experience interruptions in their work.

Limited Customization: SaaS applications are often standardized to suit a broad range of users. While this is cost-effective, it may limit customization options for specific needs.

Subscription Costs: Over time, subscription costs can add up and sometimes surpass the one-time purchase cost of traditional software. Users must carefully consider the long-term financial implications.

Vendor Lock-In: Transitioning from one SaaS provider to another can be challenging due to data and compatibility issues. This can lead to vendor lock-in, where users are tied to a specific provider.

In this ever-evolving landscape of software delivery, SaaS has become a significant player, offering numerous advantages and, at the same time, posing certain challenges that users and organizations must carefully weigh. As we delve deeper into this book, we will explore the intricacies of SaaS, its applications across different industries, and strategies for effectively utilizing this transformative software delivery model.

Chapter 2: SaaS Architecture and Infrastructure

Understanding SaaS Architecture

To grasp the essence of Software as a Service (SaaS), it's vital to delve into its architectural framework. SaaS architecture is the foundation upon which cloud-based applications are built and delivered. This chapter will provide a comprehensive understanding of SaaS architecture, its key components, and how it functions.

Key Components of SaaS Architecture:

1. *Multi-Tenancy*

At the heart of SaaS architecture lies the concept of multi-tenancy. Multi-tenancy allows a single instance of the software to serve multiple customers, or tenants, simultaneously. Each tenant's data and configuration are kept separate and secure, ensuring that one customer cannot access another's data. This shared infrastructure optimizes resource utilization, making SaaS cost-effective and efficient.

2. *Web-Based Access*

SaaS applications are accessed through web browsers, which makes them highly accessible from any device with internet connectivity. Users don't need to install or maintain software on their local devices. Instead, they simply log in through a web portal to access the application's features and functionalities.

3. *Centralized Data Storage*

In SaaS architecture, data is typically stored in centralized databases. This approach ensures data consistency, easy backups, and efficient management. It also enables collaborative work since multiple users can access and update data simultaneously.

4. Scalable Infrastructure

SaaS architecture is designed to be scalable. As the number of users and data grows, the infrastructure can easily adapt to accommodate the increased demand. This scalability allows SaaS providers to provide resources as needed and avoid underutilized infrastructure.

5. API Integration

Application Programming Interfaces (APIs) are a fundamental element of SaaS architecture. APIs enable different software systems to communicate with each other. This facilitates integration with other applications and services, allowing users to connect their SaaS applications with various tools, such as customer relationship management (CRM) systems or accounting software.

How SaaS Architecture Functions:

1. User Authentication and Authorization

When a user accesses a SaaS application, they are required to authenticate themselves by providing a username and password. Once authenticated, the system checks their access rights to determine what features and data they can access. This process is known as authorization.

2. User Interface (UI) Layer

The user interface is the front-end of a SaaS application. It's what users see and interact with. SaaS providers design user interfaces to be user-friendly, intuitive, and responsive. UI design plays a crucial role in ensuring a positive user experience.

3. Application Layer

The application layer is where the core functionality of the SaaS software resides. It includes the business logic, algorithms, and processes that drive the application's features. Users interact with this layer through the UI, triggering actions and requesting data.

4. Data Storage Layer

All user data is stored in the data storage layer. This includes user profiles, configuration settings, and the actual data managed by the application. SaaS providers implement robust data storage systems to ensure data integrity, security, and efficient retrieval.

5. Security Measures

Security is a paramount concern in SaaS architecture. To protect user data and maintain the integrity of the application, SaaS providers employ various security measures, including encryption, access controls, and data redundancy. Regular security audits and updates are essential to safeguard against evolving threats.

6. Scalability

SaaS architecture must be highly scalable to accommodate growing user bases and increasing data volumes. Scalability is achieved through a combination of hardware and software components that can be expanded to meet rising demand. This adaptability ensures that the SaaS application remains responsive and performs optimally as it scales.

7. Maintenance and Updates

SaaS providers are responsible for maintaining and updating the software. This includes implementing bug fixes, security patches, and adding new features. Maintenance and updates are typically done behind the scenes, ensuring that users always have access to the latest and most secure version of the application.

Understanding SaaS architecture is essential for both SaaS providers and users. Providers must design scalable, secure, and user-friendly architectures to deliver a seamless experience, while users can benefit from a better comprehension of how the technology they rely on daily operates. As we move forward in this exploration of SaaS, we will dive deeper into the specific aspects of SaaS architecture, such as scalability and data security, to provide a comprehensive understanding of this innovative software delivery model.

Scalability and Availability in SaaS

Scalability in SaaS:

Scalability is a fundamental aspect of SaaS architecture that underpins its ability to meet the varying demands of users and ensure consistent performance. In the context of SaaS, scalability refers to the system's capacity to handle increased workloads and data as the user base and usage grow. There are two main dimensions of scalability in SaaS: vertical scalability and horizontal scalability.

Vertical Scalability: Vertical scalability involves increasing the capacity of individual system components, such as servers, by adding more resources to them. This might mean upgrading server hardware, increasing memory, or adding more processing power to handle higher workloads.

For instance, if a SaaS application experiences a surge in users and requires more computing resources, a vertically scalable system can respond by allocating additional CPU cores or memory to the server. Vertical scalability is often limited by the physical constraints of hardware and can be more expensive as it involves upgrading existing infrastructure.

Horizontal Scalability: Horizontal scalability, on the other hand, involves adding more instances of system components, such as servers, to distribute the workload. This approach allows for easy expansion by adding more servers to the infrastructure when the system faces increased demands.

Consider a situation where a SaaS provider experiences a surge in users or data volume. Instead of upgrading existing hardware, they can add new servers to the network, distributing the load across multiple instances. Horizontal scalability is generally more cost-effective and can accommodate virtually unlimited growth.

Benefits of Scalability in SaaS:

1. Elasticity: Scalability enables the system to be elastic, meaning it can automatically adapt to fluctuating demands. This elasticity ensures that the SaaS application remains responsive even during peak usage periods and scales down when the demand decreases.

2. Improved Performance: A scalable SaaS architecture provides consistent and high performance. Users experience faster response times, reduced latency, and uninterrupted access to the application's features.

3. Cost Efficiency: Horizontal scalability can be more cost-effective in the long run. Rather than over-provisioning resources to handle occasional peak loads, SaaS providers can add resources on-demand, optimizing resource utilization and reducing unnecessary expenses.

Availability in SaaS:

SaaS providers must ensure high availability to meet the expectations of users who rely on their services for critical tasks. Availability refers to the percentage of time that a SaaS application is accessible and operational. The goal is to minimize downtime and disruptions to provide a reliable service.

Measuring Availability: Availability is typically measured as a percentage, with 100% representing continuous availability. Common availability targets include the following:

1. Five Nines (99.999%): This level of availability allows for a mere 5.26 minutes of downtime per year, making it suitable for mission-critical applications.

2. Four Nines (99.99%): This equates to approximately 52.56 minutes of downtime annually, which is acceptable for most business applications.

3. Three Nines (99.9%): Three nines availability allows for roughly 8.76 hours of downtime each year and is typically sufficient for non-critical applications.

4. Two Nines (99%): This level permits up to 3.65 days of downtime each year and is suitable for non-essential services.

Achieving High Availability:

To maintain high availability in SaaS, providers implement a combination of strategies and best practices, which may include:

1. Redundancy: SaaS providers deploy redundant components, such as servers, databases, and network connections. If one component fails, another can seamlessly take over, minimizing service interruptions.

2. Load Balancing: Load balancers distribute incoming requests across multiple servers to ensure even workloads and prevent overloading a single server.

3. Failover Systems: Failover mechanisms automatically switch to backup systems when a primary system experiences issues, maintaining service continuity.

4. Data Replication: Data is often replicated in multiple geographic locations to ensure data availability and disaster recovery.

5. Monitoring and Alerting: Continuous monitoring of system health and performance allows for quick detection and response to issues before they impact users.

6. Regular Maintenance: Scheduled maintenance is conducted during low-traffic periods to minimize user disruption.

7. Disaster Recovery Planning: SaaS providers develop comprehensive disaster recovery plans to address catastrophic events and ensure data integrity.

Challenges in Scalability and Availability:

While scalability and availability are critical for SaaS success, there are challenges that providers must navigate:

1. Complexity: Implementing scalable and highly available systems can be complex and requires careful planning, architecture, and monitoring.

2. Cost: Ensuring high availability can be expensive, as it often involves investing in redundant infrastructure and advanced monitoring and failover mechanisms.

3. Data Consistency: Maintaining data consistency across distributed systems can be a challenge, especially in horizontally scalable architectures.

4. Security: While improving availability, redundancy can also increase the potential attack surface for security threats, making robust security measures crucial.

In the world of SaaS, scalability and availability are essential components of a robust and reliable service. The ability to grow with user demands and provide consistent access ensures that SaaS applications meet user expectations and remain competitive in the market. As we continue to explore SaaS architecture and infrastructure, we will delve into other critical aspects, such as data security and regulatory compliance, to provide a comprehensive understanding of this innovative software delivery model.

Data Security and Compliance in SaaS

Data Security in SaaS:

Safeguarding sensitive data is paramount in Software as a Service (SaaS) architecture. Users trust SaaS providers with their data, and the responsibility to ensure its security falls on the shoulders of the service providers. Data security in SaaS is achieved through a combination of technical measures, policies, and procedures:

1. *Encryption*

    Encryption is a fundamental technique used to protect data in transit and at rest. SaaS providers use encryption to secure data as it moves between a user's device and the provider's servers (in transit) and when it is stored on the servers (at rest). Strong encryption algorithms, such as AES (Advanced Encryption Standard), are employed to ensure data remains confidential.

2. *Access Controls*

    SaaS providers implement access controls to restrict who can access sensitive data. This includes user authentication methods, role-based access control, and permission settings. By enforcing access controls, providers can limit data exposure to only authorized individuals.

3. *Redundancy and Backup*

    Data redundancy and backup practices are crucial for ensuring data availability and resilience. SaaS providers store data in multiple locations and create regular backups to prevent data loss due to hardware failures, disasters, or other unforeseen events.

4. *Security Audits and Testing*

    Regular security audits and testing help identify vulnerabilities and weaknesses in the SaaS infrastructure. These assessments can include penetration testing, vulnerability scanning, and code reviews. By proactively addressing security issues, providers reduce the risk of data breaches.

5. *Security Policies*

    Providers establish comprehensive security policies that govern how data is handled, including data classification, storage, and retention policies. These policies guide the behavior of both the provider's employees and the users of the SaaS application.

6. *Incident Response*

    In the event of a security incident or breach, SaaS providers must have a well-defined incident response plan in place. This plan outlines the steps to be taken to mitigate the incident, notify affected parties, and prevent further damage.

7. *User Education*

    User education is a critical aspect of data security in SaaS. Providers often offer training and resources to help users understand and practice good security habits, such as strong password management and identifying phishing attempts.

Compliance in SaaS:

SaaS providers must adhere to various regulatory requirements and industry standards to ensure the protection of user data and maintain trust. Compliance is a complex but necessary aspect of SaaS architecture:

1. *GDPR (General Data Protection Regulation)*

    The General Data Protection Regulation is a European Union regulation that governs the privacy and data protection of EU citizens. SaaS providers that handle EU citizen data must comply with GDPR, which includes obtaining user consent, providing data access and portability, and implementing strong data security measures.

2. *HIPAA (Health Insurance Portability and Accountability Act)*

    HIPAA sets the standards for the protection of sensitive healthcare data in the United States. SaaS providers in the healthcare sector must comply with HIPAA, which mandates strict controls on patient data access, transmission, and storage.

3. *SOC 2 (Service Organization Control 2)*

   SOC 2 is an auditing standard developed by the American Institute of CPAs (AICPA). It assesses the security, availability, processing integrity, confidentiality, and privacy of data within a SaaS environment. Compliance with SOC 2 demonstrates a provider's commitment to safeguarding user data.

4. *ISO 27001*

   ISO 27001 is an international standard for information security management systems (ISMS). SaaS providers that achieve ISO 27001 certification demonstrate their commitment to maintaining the highest levels of security and protecting sensitive information.

5. *PCI DSS (Payment Card Industry Data Security Standard)*

   SaaS providers that handle credit card payments must comply with PCI DSS. This standard ensures secure payment processing by implementing measures to protect cardholder data and prevent data breaches.

6. *Industry-Specific Regulations*

   SaaS providers operating in specific industries, such as finance or education, may need to adhere to industry-specific regulations and standards that address data security and privacy concerns.

Challenges in Data Security and Compliance:

Ensuring data security and compliance in SaaS presents several challenges:

1. *Evolving Regulations*

    Regulatory requirements are subject to change and can vary across different regions, making it challenging for SaaS providers to stay up to date and in compliance.

2. *Data Residency*

    Data residency laws in various countries dictate where data can be stored and processed. Providers must navigate these requirements to ensure they are not inadvertently violating regulations.

3. *User Privacy Concerns*

    SaaS users are increasingly concerned about their data privacy. Providers must address these concerns to build and maintain user trust.

4. *Resource Intensity*

    Achieving and maintaining compliance can be resource-intensive, as it requires ongoing investments in security measures, audits, and documentation.

5. *Global Operations*

    SaaS providers with a global user base must understand and adhere to the various data protection regulations that apply to their users, regardless of their location.

Data security and compliance are non-negotiable aspects of SaaS architecture. Providers must prioritize the protection of user data and adhere to relevant regulations and standards to maintain user trust and operate within the boundaries of the law. As we continue to explore SaaS architecture and infrastructure, we will delve into other critical aspects, such as data privacy and regulatory challenges specific to different industries.

Chapter 3: Building a SaaS Product

Ideation and Conceptualization

The journey of creating a Software as a Service (SaaS) product begins with ideation and conceptualization. In this critical phase, the foundation of your SaaS product takes shape, and its success hinges on your ability to identify a problem, generate innovative solutions, and map out the initial plan. Let's dive into the essential steps and considerations of ideation and conceptualization in the SaaS product development process.

1. *Identifying a Problem or Need*

Successful SaaS products often start with a clear identification of a problem or unmet need. Understanding your target audience and their pain points is the key to finding a compelling problem worth solving. Here's how to approach it:

- Market Research: Study the market, industry trends, and competitor landscape. Look for gaps and opportunities where your SaaS product can excel.

- User Interviews: Talk to potential users to uncover their challenges and frustrations. Listen to their experiences, preferences, and desires.

- Data Analysis: Analyze relevant data, such as user behavior or industry reports, to identify trends and areas where improvement is needed.

- User Personas: Create user personas to gain a deeper understanding of your target audience. Personas represent your ideal users and help you empathize with their specific problems.

2. Generating Innovative Solutions

Once you've pinpointed a problem or need, it's time to brainstorm innovative solutions. The goal is to come up with ideas that are not only creative but also feasible and aligned with your target audience's requirements. Here's how to foster innovation:

- Brainstorming Sessions: Organize brainstorming sessions with your team or collaborators to generate a wide range of ideas. Encourage open and free-thinking discussions.

- Ideation Frameworks: Utilize ideation frameworks such as "Design Thinking" or "Innovation Games" to structure your creative process and encourage fresh perspectives.

- Idea Validation: Test your ideas with potential users, stakeholders, or experts to gather feedback and validate their feasibility and appeal.

- User-Centered Design: Prioritize user-centered design principles to ensure that your solutions address real user needs.

3. Defining Your SaaS Product

With a clear problem in mind and innovative solutions on the table, the next step is to define your SaaS product. This includes shaping its core features, functionalities, and purpose. To do this effectively:

- Minimum Viable Product (MVP): Consider building an MVP, which is a simplified version of your product that includes the most essential features. MVPs are valuable for testing the market and gathering early feedback.

- Feature Prioritization: Determine which features are critical for your product's core functionality and prioritize them over additional, non-essential features.

- Use Cases and User Stories: Develop use cases and user stories that describe how users will interact with your product. These narratives provide a clear understanding of user experiences.

- Technical Specifications: Work with your development team to define the technical specifications and requirements needed to bring your product to life.

4. *Market Research and Validation*

Market research and validation are crucial components of ideation and conceptualization. They help you confirm the demand for your product and ensure it aligns with market realities:

- Competitive Analysis: Revisit your competitive landscape to understand how your SaaS product compares with existing solutions. Identify your unique value proposition.

- Prototyping: Create prototypes or mockups of your product to visualize how it will look and function. These prototypes can be used for user testing and investor presentations.

- User Feedback: Continuously gather feedback from potential users to fine-tune your product concept. Make necessary adjustments based on user insights.

- Market Fit: Evaluate the product-market fit by examining how well your solution addresses the identified problem and resonates with your target audience.

5. Business Model and Monetization Strategy

As part of the conceptualization process, you need to define your business model and how you plan to monetize your SaaS product. This includes considering pricing, revenue streams, and sustainability:

- Pricing Strategy: Determine the pricing model that best suits your product, whether it's a subscription-based model, a freemium model, or something else. Consider pricing tiers and options.

- Revenue Projections: Create financial projections that estimate your potential revenue streams based on different user acquisition scenarios.

- Sustainability: Assess how your business model and pricing strategy can ensure the long-term sustainability of your SaaS product.

6. Creating a Conceptual Roadmap

A conceptual roadmap outlines the high-level plan for your SaaS product. While not as detailed as a development roadmap, it provides a visual guide to help your team and stakeholders understand the product's direction:

- Milestones: Identify key milestones, such as product launch, beta testing, and major feature releases.

- Timeline: Create a rough timeline that outlines when you expect to reach each milestone. This timeline can be adjusted as your product progresses.

- Dependencies: Highlight dependencies between different stages of development and areas that need attention for the project to move forward.

The ideation and conceptualization phase is where your SaaS product journey truly begins. By carefully identifying problems, generating innovative solutions, and defining the product concept, you set the stage for the subsequent development and execution phases. In the chapters that follow, we'll delve into the practical aspects of building, launching, and scaling your SaaS product.

Designing the User Experience (UX)

Designing the user experience (UX) is a critical aspect of developing a successful Software as a Service (SaaS) product. The user experience encompasses the way users interact with your product, the satisfaction they derive from it, and their ability to achieve their goals efficiently and effectively. In this chapter, we'll explore the key principles, processes, and considerations involved in creating an exceptional UX for your SaaS product:

1. *User-Centered Design*

User-centered design is the foundation of a great user experience. This approach places the user at the center of the design process, ensuring that the product is tailored to their needs and preferences. Key principles of user-centered design include:

- User Research: Conduct extensive user research to understand your target audience, their goals, pain points, and behavior. This can involve surveys, interviews, and usability testing.

- User Personas: Create user personas that represent the different types of users who will interact with your product. Personas help you empathize with your users and make design decisions that cater to their specific needs.

- Prototyping: Develop interactive prototypes and wireframes to visualize the user interface and gather early feedback. Prototyping allows you to test design concepts and refine them before development.

- Iterative Design: Follow an iterative design process, making incremental improvements based on user feedback and usability testing. Continuously refine and optimize the user experience.

2. User Interface (UI) Design

UI design focuses on the visual and interactive elements of your SaaS product. It includes the layout, color schemes, typography, and overall aesthetics that influence how users perceive and navigate the application. Effective UI design should:

- Prioritize Clarity: Ensure that the user interface is clear and intuitive. Labels, buttons, and navigation elements should be easy to understand.

- Consistency: Maintain consistency in design elements across the product. This includes using a consistent color palette, typography, and layout to create a cohesive look and feel.

- Responsiveness: Design for responsiveness to accommodate users accessing the product on various devices and screen sizes. A responsive design ensures a seamless experience across platforms.

- Accessibility: Make your SaaS product accessible to users with disabilities. This involves implementing features like alt text for images and ensuring keyboard navigation is available.

3. Information Architecture

Information architecture focuses on the organization and structure of content within your SaaS product. It plays a crucial role in helping users find the information and features they need. Key considerations include:

- Navigation: Design a clear and intuitive navigation system that guides users to different parts of the product. This may involve menus, sidebars, or search functionalities.

- Content Hierarchy: Organize content in a hierarchical manner, with the most important information and features easily accessible. A well-defined content hierarchy helps users quickly locate what they need.

- Labels and Categories: Use clear and descriptive labels for content and features. Create categories or sections that group related information together.

4. *User Flows*

User flows are visual representations of the paths users take to complete specific tasks or achieve goals within your SaaS product. Understanding and optimizing these flows is essential for a smooth and efficient user experience. To create effective user flows:

- Identify Key Tasks: Define the primary tasks or goals that users want to accomplish within your product. This could include signing up, making a purchase, or creating content.

- Map User Paths: Create diagrams or flowcharts that outline the steps users must take to achieve these goals. This helps you identify potential bottlenecks and optimize the flow.

- Remove Friction: Identify and eliminate any unnecessary steps or barriers that may hinder users from completing their tasks. The goal is to create a streamlined and frictionless experience.

5. *Usability Testing*

Usability testing is a critical step in the UX design process. It involves observing real users as they interact with your SaaS product to identify usability issues and gather feedback. To conduct effective usability testing:

- Define Test Scenarios: Determine specific scenarios or tasks that you want users to complete during the test. For example, you might ask a user to sign up for an account or locate a particular feature.

- Recruit Participants: Find representative users who match your target audience. Participants should be unfamiliar with the product to ensure unbiased feedback.

- Observe and Collect Feedback: Watch users as they complete the tasks and take notes on their interactions, pain points, and comments. After the test, gather additional feedback through surveys or interviews.

- Iterative Improvements: Use the insights gained from usability testing to make iterative improvements to the user interface and overall user experience.

6. *Mobile Responsiveness*

With the prevalence of mobile devices, ensuring that your SaaS product is mobile-responsive is essential. Mobile responsiveness means that your product functions and looks good on smartphones and tablets. Consider the following:

- Mobile-First Design: Begin the design process by focusing on the mobile experience. This approach ensures that your product is optimized for smaller screens and touch interactions.

- Responsive Design Frameworks: Utilize responsive design frameworks and tools to create adaptable layouts and user interfaces that adjust to different screen sizes.

- Mobile App Consideration: Decide whether your SaaS product should also have a dedicated mobile app. If so, design and develop it to provide a seamless and native mobile experience.

Creating a remarkable user experience for your SaaS product is a multifaceted endeavor that requires a deep understanding of your users, meticulous attention to design, and ongoing iteration and improvement. By placing the user at the center of your design process and following best practices in UI/UX, you can build a product that not only meets user expectations but also delights and retains your audience. In the chapters that follow, we'll explore the development and testing phases that bring your SaaS product to life.

Development and Testing

In the journey of building a Software as a Service (SaaS) product, the development and testing phases are pivotal in turning your ideas and designs into a functional and reliable software solution. These stages involve coding, infrastructure setup, and rigorous testing to ensure that your SaaS product is robust and ready for deployment. Let's delve into the key aspects and considerations of the development and testing phases.

Development Phase:

1. *Coding and Development*

The coding and development phase is where the actual construction of your SaaS product takes place. It involves writing the software code that brings your product's features to life. Key aspects of this phase include:

- Framework Selection: Choose the appropriate development framework or stack based on your project's requirements. Consider factors like scalability, technology stack familiarity, and your development team's expertise.

- Agile Development: Adopt agile development methodologies to enable iterative and flexible development. Agile practices like Scrum or Kanban can help you manage tasks, prioritize features, and adapt to changing requirements.

- Version Control: Implement version control systems, such as Git, to manage your codebase and collaborate with other developers effectively. Version control allows you to track changes, resolve conflicts, and maintain code consistency.

- Continuous Integration: Set up continuous integration and continuous deployment (CI/CD) pipelines to automate testing and deployment processes. CI/CD ensures that code changes are regularly integrated, tested, and deployed to production environments.

2. *Database Design and Implementation*

The design and implementation of your database are crucial for storing and managing data efficiently. Consider the following aspects:

- Database Selection: Choose the appropriate type of database (SQL, NoSQL) based on the nature of your data and scalability requirements. Popular databases include MySQL, PostgreSQL, MongoDB, and Redis.

- Schema Design: Define the database schema to structure and organize data logically. Determine the relationships between different data entities.

- Indexing: Implement indexing to improve query performance. Indexes speed up data retrieval by allowing the database to quickly locate specific records.

- Scalability: Plan for database scalability by considering replication, sharding, or caching strategies that can handle increasing data loads.

3. *Security Implementation*

Security is a paramount concern during the development phase. Implementing robust security measures helps protect your SaaS product from vulnerabilities and threats. Key security aspects include:

- Authentication and Authorization: Set up authentication and authorization mechanisms to ensure that only authorized users can access specific parts of your product.

- Data Encryption: Implement data encryption to protect sensitive information both in transit and at rest. Encryption protocols like SSL/TLS and AES are common choices.

- Cross-Site Scripting (XSS) and Cross-Site Request Forgery (CSRF) Prevention: Apply security measures to prevent common web application vulnerabilities, such as XSS and CSRF attacks.

- Regular Security Audits: Conduct regular security audits and vulnerability assessments to identify and address potential weaknesses in your product.

Testing Phase:

1. *Unit Testing*

Unit testing is the first line of defense in the testing phase. It focuses on verifying the functionality of individual code units, such as functions or methods. Key unit testing aspects include:

- Test Frameworks: Choose unit testing frameworks like JUnit (for Java), pytest (for Python), or Mocha (for JavaScript) to create and run unit tests.

- Test Coverage: Aim for high test coverage, ensuring that a significant portion of your codebase is tested. Code coverage tools help identify untested or poorly tested areas.

- Continuous Integration: Integrate unit tests into your CI/CD pipeline to automatically run tests with every code change. This ensures that new code doesn't introduce regressions.

2. *Integration Testing*

Integration testing evaluates the interactions between different components, services, or modules within your SaaS product. Key aspects of integration testing include:

- Test Scenarios: Define integration test scenarios that cover the interactions between components, including data flow and communication between services.

- Mocking and Stubs: Use mocking and stubbing techniques to simulate the behavior of external dependencies or services that your product relies on.

- Data Migration: If applicable, test data migration processes to ensure that data is transferred correctly when transitioning from development to production environments.

3. *User Acceptance Testing (UAT)*

User acceptance testing involves verifying that your SaaS product meets user expectations and performs as intended. UAT is typically conducted by actual users or stakeholders. Key UAT aspects include:

- Test Cases: Develop UAT test cases that align with user scenarios and real-world usage. These cases should mimic how users will interact with the product.

- Feedback Collection: Gather feedback from UAT participants to identify issues, usability concerns, and any discrepancies between the product and user expectations.

- Regression Testing: Perform regression testing to ensure that any changes made as a result of UAT do not introduce new defects or regressions.

4. *Performance and Load Testing*

Performance and load testing assess how your SaaS product behaves under different conditions and loads. It helps identify performance bottlenecks and scalability issues. Key aspects of performance testing include:

- Scalability Testing: Assess the product's ability to handle increased user loads. This may involve simulating a growing user base and monitoring system performance.

- Load Testing Tools: Use load testing tools like Apache JMeter, Gatling, or Locust to simulate various user activities and measure the product's response under load.

- Stress Testing: Push the product to its limits to determine how it behaves under extreme conditions, including peak traffic and resource constraints.

5. *Security Testing*

Security testing is essential to identify and address vulnerabilities and threats that could compromise your SaaS product. Key security testing aspects include:

- Vulnerability Scanning: Conduct vulnerability scanning and penetration testing to identify and address security weaknesses in your product.

- Code Review: Perform code reviews with a focus on security considerations, identifying and fixing issues like SQL injection, cross-site scripting, and authentication vulnerabilities.

- Compliance Testing: Verify that your product complies with industry-specific regulations and standards, such as HIPAA, GDPR, or PCI DSS.

The development and testing phases are crucial for turning your SaaS product concept into a functional and reliable solution. Robust development practices, security implementation, and comprehensive testing ensure that your product meets user expectations and operates smoothly. In the upcoming chapters, we'll explore deployment, monitoring, and scaling to prepare your SaaS product for the market.

Chapter 4: SaaS Pricing Models

Subscription-Based Pricing

SaaS pricing models are the financial foundation of your Software as a Service (SaaS) product. They play a pivotal role in determining how your product generates revenue and how it is perceived by customers. One of the most popular and widely adopted SaaS pricing models is subscription-based pricing. In this chapter, we'll explore the intricacies of subscription-based pricing, its advantages, challenges, and the key considerations for implementing it effectively.

Understanding Subscription-Based Pricing

Subscription-based pricing, often referred to as the subscription model, is a pricing strategy where customers pay a recurring fee at regular intervals to access and use a SaaS product. The intervals can vary, with common options including monthly, quarterly, and annually. This pricing model has gained immense popularity in the SaaS industry due to its flexibility, predictability, and alignment with the SaaS delivery model.

Advantages of Subscription-Based Pricing

1. **Predictable Revenue:** One of the primary advantages of subscription-based pricing is the predictability of revenue. With recurring payments, you can forecast and plan your finances more accurately, which is particularly advantageous for budgeting, resource allocation, and growth planning.

2. **Steady Customer Relationships:** Subscriptions foster ongoing relationships with customers. As long as they find value in your product, they are likely to continue their subscriptions, leading to improved customer retention and loyalty.

3. **Lower Barrier to Entry:** Monthly or quarterly subscription payments often have a lower upfront cost compared to one-time purchases or other pricing models. This makes it easier for potential customers to try out your product.

4. **Flexible Tiered Pricing:** Subscription-based pricing allows for tiered or segmented pricing models, where different plans or tiers offer various features and levels of service. Customers can choose the plan that aligns with their needs and budget.

5. **Regular Updates and Support:** With a reliable stream of revenue, you can invest in product development, regular updates, and exceptional customer support, which further enhances the customer experience.

Challenges of Subscription-Based Pricing

1. **Customer Churn:** The downside of subscriptions is that customers can cancel or "churn" at any time. Churn rates can affect revenue stability, so it's important to manage customer relationships and continually improve the product.

2. **Acquisition Costs:** Acquiring new customers can be costly, and it may take some time to recoup those acquisition costs through subscription revenue.

3. **Competitive Market:** In a competitive SaaS market, you need to differentiate your product and continually prove its value to retain customers.

4. **Pricing Complexity:** Creating and managing multiple subscription tiers with different features can be complex and may require careful pricing strategy and ongoing analysis.

Key Considerations for Effective Subscription-Based Pricing

1. **Pricing Tiers:** Define clear pricing tiers that align with customer needs and expectations. Each tier should offer increasing value and functionality to incentivize users to upgrade.

2. **Value-Based Pricing:** Consider the value your product provides to different customer segments. Pricing should reflect this value while remaining competitive in the market.

3. **Trial Periods:** Offer trial periods or a "freemium" model, allowing users to experience your product before committing to a subscription.

4. **Renewal and Churn Analysis:** Continually monitor customer renewal rates and churn rates. Identify reasons for churn and develop strategies to reduce it.

5. **Pricing Optimization:** Regularly assess and optimize your pricing model. Adjust pricing tiers, features, and intervals based on market feedback, competitor pricing, and evolving customer needs.

6. **Discounts and Promotions:** Use discounts or promotions strategically to attract new customers, encourage upgrades, or retain existing customers.

7. **Clear Communication:** Transparently communicate pricing details, including any potential price increases, to customers. Avoid unexpected cost shocks.

8. **Customer Engagement:** Engage with your customers to understand their needs and gather feedback. This can help you tailor your subscription plans to better serve them.

Examples of Subscription-Based Pricing

Several well-known SaaS products employ subscription-based pricing models:

1. **Microsoft 365:** Microsoft 365 offers monthly or annual subscriptions for its suite of productivity tools, including Word, Excel, and PowerPoint.

2. **Adobe Creative Cloud:** Adobe's Creative Cloud subscription model provides access to creative software like Photoshop and Illustrator on a monthly or annual basis.

3. **HubSpot:** HubSpot offers subscription-based pricing for its marketing, sales, and customer service software, with different tiers catering to various business needs.

4. **Slack:** Slack's subscription model charges per active user, providing businesses with communication and collaboration tools.

5. **Spotify:** Spotify, a music streaming service, offers premium subscriptions that remove ads and provide offline listening for a monthly fee.

Conclusion

Subscription-based pricing is a versatile and effective model for SaaS products, offering a balance of predictable revenue, customer relationships, and accessible pricing for users. By carefully defining pricing tiers, focusing on value-based pricing, and regularly optimizing your model, you can harness the benefits of subscription pricing while mitigating its challenges. In the next chapter, we'll explore alternative pricing models that cater to different SaaS product strategies and customer preferences.

Freemium and Tiered Pricing

SaaS pricing models are a critical component of a successful Software as a Service (SaaS) product strategy. Two popular pricing models that have gained traction in the SaaS industry are freemium and tiered pricing. In this chapter, we'll explore these models, their advantages, challenges, and key considerations for implementing them effectively.

Freemium Pricing Model

The freemium pricing model is characterized by offering a free, basic version of your SaaS product while charging for premium features, additional capabilities, or an enhanced experience. This approach allows users to get a taste of your product's core functionality without an upfront financial commitment. Let's dive into the nuances of the freemium model.

Advantages of Freemium Pricing

1. **User Acquisition:** Freemium models are excellent for user acquisition. They lower the barrier to entry, attracting a larger user base that can convert to paying customers over time.

2. **Product Visibility:** Offering a free version of your product can increase its visibility and generate word-of-mouth marketing, creating a buzz around your brand.

3. **User Engagement:** Free users can become engaged users. By using your product over time, they may realize its value and consider upgrading to a premium version for additional benefits.

4. **Upselling Opportunities:** The freemium model provides opportunities to upsell users to premium plans. Once free users see the value in your product, they may be more inclined to pay for extra features.

5. **Market Insights:** Freemium models offer valuable market insights by tracking how free users interact with your product. This data can inform product development and marketing strategies.

Challenges of Freemium Pricing

1. **Monetization Challenge:** Convincing free users to upgrade to paid plans can be challenging. A substantial portion of free users may never convert.

2. **Balancing Act:** Striking the right balance between what's offered for free and what's locked behind a paywall is essential. If too much is given away for free, revenue may suffer.

3. **Support Costs:** Providing customer support for free users can be resource-intensive, especially if they require assistance but don't generate direct revenue.

4. **Usage Costs:** High usage of free resources, such as storage or server capacity, can result in substantial costs without a corresponding increase in revenue.

5. **Competition:** In highly competitive markets, free users may be more inclined to switch to a different product that offers similar features for free.

Key Considerations for Effective Freemium Pricing

1. **Clear Value Proposition:** Ensure that the free version of your product provides a clear and valuable solution to a specific problem. Users should see immediate benefits.

2. **Premium Features:** Clearly define what premium features or benefits users gain by upgrading to a paid plan. Make the added value enticing.

3. **Conversion Strategies:** Implement strategies to convert free users into paying customers. This might involve in-app messages, email campaigns, or trial periods for premium features.

4. **Support Strategy:** Develop a support strategy for free users that balances their needs with cost considerations. Consider offering premium support as part of paid plans.

5. **Usage Limits:** Set reasonable limits on the usage of free resources to control costs and prevent abuse while still providing value.

Tiered Pricing Model

Tiered pricing, also known as a pricing ladder, involves offering multiple subscription plans at different price points, each with distinct features and levels of service. Customers can choose the plan that best aligns with their needs and budget. Let's explore the ins and outs of the tiered pricing model.

Advantages of Tiered Pricing

1. **Catering to Diverse Needs:** Tiered pricing caters to a diverse range of customer needs. It allows you to target various segments of the market, from individual users to enterprises.

2. **Maximized Revenue:** By offering a range of plans, you maximize revenue potential. Customers who need more features or higher usage limits are willing to pay a premium for those benefits.

3. **Scalable Growth:** As customers' needs grow, they can easily upgrade to a higher-tier plan. This scalable growth benefits both customers and your revenue stream.

4. **Competitive Edge:** Offering tiered plans makes your product more competitive by accommodating customers with varying requirements. This can set you apart from single-plan competitors.

5. **Customer Retention:** As customers' needs change, they can switch between plans, keeping them engaged with your product rather than seeking alternatives.

Challenges of Tiered Pricing

1. **Complexity:** Managing multiple pricing tiers can be complex. Balancing feature sets, pricing points, and customer expectations can be challenging.

2. **Decision Fatigue:** Customers may experience decision fatigue when presented with numerous plan options. This can lead to hesitation or abandonment.

3. **Segmentation Accuracy:** Accurate segmentation is crucial. Misclassifying customers or offering plans that don't align with actual needs can deter potential buyers.

4. **Communication:** Clearly communicating the differences between pricing tiers is essential to prevent misunderstandings and potential frustration.

5. **Price Point Strategy:** Determining the right price points for each tier can be challenging. It requires market research, competitor analysis, and an understanding of your product's value.

Key Considerations for Effective Tiered Pricing

1. **Feature Sets:** Define distinct feature sets for each pricing tier, ensuring that each plan offers increasing value as users move up the ladder.

2. **Pricing Strategy:** Develop a pricing strategy that considers the perceived value of features, competitive pricing, and the willingness of customers to pay for additional benefits.

3. **Segmentation:** Accurately segment your customer base to understand their needs, behaviors, and preferences. Tailor pricing tiers to these segments.

4. **Communication:** Clearly communicate the benefits and differences between each tier through your marketing materials and on your pricing page.

5. **Flexibility:** Allow customers to easily upgrade or downgrade their plans as their needs change, preventing churn and improving retention.

The freemium and tiered pricing models offer flexibility in attracting a wide range of customers and revenue streams. To leverage these models effectively, focus on clear value propositions, effective conversion strategies, and the right balance between free and premium features for freemium pricing. For tiered pricing, carefully craft feature sets, develop a sound pricing strategy, and tailor your communication to match customer segments. In the next chapter, we'll explore other pricing models that cater to specific business strategies and customer preferences.

Usage-Based Pricing Models

Usage-based pricing models are gaining prominence as they offer a dynamic and flexible way to charge customers based on their actual usage of the SaaS product. In this chapter, we'll delve into the intricacies of usage-based pricing models, their advantages, challenges, and key considerations for their effective implementation.

Understanding Usage-Based Pricing Models

Usage-based pricing models are based on the idea that customers pay for the SaaS product according to how much they use it. The pricing structure typically involves charging customers for the number of specific actions, transactions, or resources they consume within the product. It provides a flexible approach that can be attractive to both customers and SaaS providers.

Advantages of Usage-Based Pricing Models

1. **Cost Efficiency:** Customers appreciate the cost-efficiency of usage-based pricing as they only pay for what they use. This aligns well with the "pay as you go" mentality.

2. **Scalability:** The model is inherently scalable, allowing customers to scale their usage up or down as their needs change, which leads to customer satisfaction.

3. **Fairness:** Usage-based pricing ensures fairness as customers pay proportionally to their actual usage. This eliminates overpaying for unused features or capacity.

4. **Encourages Adoption:** The model encourages broader product adoption, as there is less risk in trying new features or scaling up the usage.

5. **Data-Driven Insights:** Usage-based pricing models generate valuable data on how customers engage with the product. This data can inform product improvements and marketing strategies.

Challenges of Usage-Based Pricing Models

1. **Complexity:** Managing and calculating usage-based billing can be complex, especially if there are numerous usage metrics or different pricing tiers.

2. **Customer Predictability:** Usage-based pricing makes it challenging for customers to predict their monthly expenses. This lack of predictability can be a drawback for some businesses.

3. **Pricing Transparency:** Ensuring transparency in pricing and billing is vital. Complex usage metrics and billing calculations can lead to confusion and disputes.

4. **Competitive Positioning:** In highly competitive markets, pricing transparency and aligning usage-based costs with the perceived value of the product are crucial.

5. **Monetization Balance:** Striking a balance between fair pricing and profitability can be challenging. Ensuring that usage-based pricing covers operational costs and generates profit is a delicate task

Key Considerations for Effective Usage-Based Pricing

1. **Clear Usage Metrics:** Define clear and understandable usage metrics that are closely aligned with the value that customers derive from the product. Metrics should be transparent and easy to track.

2. **Pricing Tiers:** Offer multiple pricing tiers with different usage limits and pricing points to cater to a range of customers, from small businesses to large enterprises.

3. **Usage Monitoring:** Invest in robust usage monitoring and billing systems to accurately track customer usage and generate clear and accurate invoices.

4. **Predictable Pricing:** While usage-based pricing offers flexibility, consider introducing plans or features that provide some level of predictability for customers who prefer it.

5. **Customer Education:** Educate customers about the advantages of usage-based pricing, showing how it can save them money and allow for scalability.

Examples of Usage-Based Pricing Models

1. **Amazon Web Services (AWS):** AWS offers usage-based pricing for various cloud services, charging customers based on resources used, such as storage, compute power, or data transfer.

2. **Twilio:** Twilio, a cloud communications platform, utilizes a usage-based model where customers are charged based on the number of calls, messages, or other communications made through the platform.

3. **Stripe:** Stripe, a payment processing platform, employs a usage-based pricing model by charging customers based on the number of transactions processed.

4. **Zoom:** Zoom, a popular video conferencing platform, has a usage-based pricing structure where customers pay based on the number of participants and meeting duration.

5. **Google Cloud Platform (GCP):** GCP offers a range of services with usage-based pricing, allowing customers to pay for the compute power, storage, and data usage they require.

Usage-based pricing models offer a dynamic approach to SaaS pricing, providing cost-efficiency and scalability. However, they also introduce complexity, cost transparency challenges, and a need for effective customer education. By defining clear usage metrics, offering pricing tiers, investing in usage monitoring, and providing some level of predictability, businesses can harness the benefits of usage-based pricing models. In the next chapter, we'll explore other pricing models that cater to different aspects of customer preferences and business strategies.

Chapter 5: SaaS Sales and Marketing Strategies

Target Audience and Market Research

In the world of Software as a Service (SaaS), a product is only as good as its ability to reach the right audience. You can have the most powerful, feature-rich SaaS solution, but without an effective sales and marketing strategy, your efforts may be in vain. In this chapter, we will delve into the critical aspects of targeting the right audience and conducting thorough market research to ensure your SaaS venture's success.

Identifying Your Target Audience

The success of your SaaS business begins with a clear understanding of your target audience. Without a well-defined audience, your marketing efforts risk being scattered, and your sales team may struggle to convert leads into customers. To identify your target audience, consider the following steps:

1. **Customer Personas**: Start by creating detailed customer personas. These personas should reflect the characteristics of your ideal customers. What industries are they in? What are their job roles? What are their pain points, challenges, and goals? The more detailed your personas, the better you can tailor your marketing efforts to their specific needs.

2. **Data Analysis**: Leverage data analysis to understand your existing customer base. Identify patterns and commonalities among your current customers. What industries or verticals are most represented? What features or functionalities do they use most frequently? This data can help you pinpoint your core customer segments.

3. **Competitor Analysis**: Study your competitors and their customer base. This can provide valuable insights into the types of customers who are most likely to engage with your SaaS product. You can identify gaps in the market where your product could be particularly appealing.

4. **Surveys and Feedback**: Don't underestimate the power of direct feedback. Conduct surveys and solicit feedback from your existing customers. This can help you uncover their pain points and expectations, guiding your efforts to attract similar prospects.

5. **Market Trends**: Keep an eye on industry and market trends. As the market evolves, so do customer preferences and needs. Staying attuned to these trends can help you adapt your target audience over time.

Conducting Market Research

With a clear picture of your target audience, you can then move on to conducting comprehensive market research. Market research is essential for understanding the competitive landscape, positioning your product, and making informed marketing decisions. Here's how to go about it:

1. **Competitive Analysis**: Start by examining your competitors. What other SaaS solutions are available in your niche? Analyze their features, pricing, and customer base. Identify their strengths and weaknesses to find opportunities for differentiation.

2. **SWOT Analysis**: Perform a SWOT analysis for your SaaS product. This involves evaluating your product's Strengths, Weaknesses, Opportunities, and Threats. Knowing your product's strengths and weaknesses helps you identify areas for improvement, while recognizing opportunities and threats enables you to refine your marketing strategy.

3. **Market Size and Growth**: Determine the size of your target market and its growth potential. This data helps you set realistic goals and understand the

scope of your business. Is the market large enough to sustain your growth ambitions?

4. **Customer Needs and Pain Points**: Understand the specific needs and pain points of your target audience. What problems can your SaaS product solve for them? Market research can reveal unmet needs and opportunities for innovation.

5. **Pricing Strategies**: Research pricing strategies within your market. Pricing plays a critical role in attracting customers. Analyze the pricing models of your competitors and consider which approach aligns with your product and target audience.

6. **Regulatory and Compliance Factors**: Be aware of any regulatory or compliance factors that may impact your SaaS product. Depending on your target industry, there may be specific regulations to adhere to, and understanding these is crucial for success.

7. **Technology Trends**: Stay current with technology trends that may affect your market. For example, the adoption of cloud computing, AI, or block-chain can impact the demand for certain SaaS solutions.

8. **Customer Feedback and Surveys**: Continuously gather customer feedback through surveys and other forms of communication. This feedback can help you refine your product, customer support, and marketing strategies based on real customer experiences.

Tailoring Your Marketing and Sales Approach

Once you've identified your target audience and conducted thorough market research, it's time to tailor your marketing and sales approach to maximize your chances of success. Here are some strategies to consider:

1. **Content Marketing**: Create content that speaks directly to the pain points and needs of your target audience. Blog posts, ebooks, webinars, and videos can position your brand as an authority in your niche.

2. **Social Media Marketing**: Use social media platforms to connect with your audience. Share valuable content, engage in conversations, and leverage targeted advertising to reach your ideal customers.

3. **Email Marketing**: Craft personalized email campaigns that cater to the interests and preferences of your target audience. Segment your email list based on customer personas and behavioral data.

4. **SEO and SEM**: Optimize your website for search engines (SEO) to ensure your SaaS product ranks well for relevant keywords. Complement this with search engine marketing (SEM) to capture high-intent leads.

5. **Partnerships and Alliances**: Explore partnerships with companies that share your target audience. Joint marketing efforts and co-branded initiatives can expand your reach.

6. **Product Positioning**: Clearly define the unique value propositions of your SaaS product. Highlight how it addresses the specific needs of your target audience.

7. **Sales Enablement**: Equip your sales team with the tools and knowledge needed to engage effectively with your audience. Provide them with the content and insights required to convert leads into customers.

8. **Customer Retention**: Don't forget about existing customers. Implement strategies for customer retention, including ongoing support, feature updates, and loyalty programs.

In conclusion, identifying your target audience and conducting thorough market research are foundational steps in building a successful SaaS business. With a clear understanding of your audience's needs and a comprehensive grasp of the market, you can tailor your marketing and sales strategies to attract, convert, and retain customers. Stay agile, adapt to market changes, and consistently refine your approach to ensure your SaaS venture's long-term growth and prosperity.

Creating an Effective Sales Funnel

In the ever-evolving realm of Software as a Service (SaaS), the journey from a lead to a paying customer is a carefully orchestrated process. An essential component of this process is the sales funnel, a strategic framework that guides potential customers through various stages of awareness, consideration, and decision-making. In this chapter, we explore how to create an effective sales funnel that can transform prospects into loyal SaaS subscribers.

Understanding the Sales Funnel

Before delving into the specifics of building an effective sales funnel, it's important to grasp the fundamental concept of the sales funnel itself. This framework is a visual representation of the customer journey, divided into distinct stages, each with its unique objectives. The most common stages include:

1. **Awareness**: At the top of the funnel, the goal is to make potential customers aware of your SaaS solution. This is often achieved through marketing efforts such as content marketing, social media, and advertising.

2. **Interest**: In this stage, you aim to pique the interest of those who have become aware of your SaaS product. Provide valuable information and solutions to their pain points to keep them engaged.

3. **Consideration**: Once prospects are interested, they enter the consideration stage. Here, they evaluate your SaaS offering in more detail, comparing it to alternatives and assessing how it aligns with their needs.

4. **Decision**: The decision stage is where prospects decide whether to become paying customers. Your goal is to convince them that your SaaS solution is the best choice for them.

5. **Action**: After the decision is made, prospects take action, becoming customers by signing up, making a purchase, or subscribing to your SaaS product.

Building Your Sales Funnel

Creating an effective sales funnel requires careful planning and execution. Here are the key steps to construct a successful funnel:

1. Define Your Target Audience: Your sales funnel must be tailored to your specific audience. To do this, refer to the customer personas created in the previous chapter. The more you understand your audience, the better you can address their needs at each stage of the funnel.

2. Develop a Value Proposition: At the awareness stage, it's crucial to communicate your SaaS product's unique value proposition. Why should potential customers choose your solution over others? This is the first step in capturing their attention.

3. Create Awareness: Use marketing strategies like content marketing, social media, and search engine optimization (SEO) to create awareness among your target audience. Content should align with the interests and pain points of your audience to draw them in.

4. Nurture Leads: As potential customers move from awareness to interest, engage them with informative content and resources. Email marketing, webinars, and free trials are effective tools for nurturing leads and keeping them interested.

5. Offer Educational Content: During the consideration stage, provide educational content that helps prospects make informed decisions. This content should highlight the specific benefits of your SaaS solution and demonstrate how it can address their needs.

6. Implement Lead Scoring: Lead scoring is a valuable tactic to identify leads that are most likely to convert. Assign scores based on engagement and behavior, allowing your sales team to prioritize their efforts.

7. Engage with Prospects: Personalize your interactions with prospects, offering one-on-one demos, consultations, or answers to their specific questions. This tailored approach can help move them from the consideration stage to the decision stage.

8. Provide Social Proof: At the decision stage, prospects are looking for assurance that your SaaS product is a reliable choice. Share testimonials, case studies, and reviews to demonstrate your product's value.

9. Simplify the Conversion Process: Make it as easy as possible for prospects to take action. Whether it's signing up for a free trial, starting a subscription, or making a purchase, the process should be streamlined and intuitive.

10. Retention Strategies: The sales funnel doesn't end with a conversion. Continue to engage with customers, providing ongoing support, updates, and additional value to retain their loyalty.

11. Analyze and Refine: Regularly analyze your sales funnel to identify bottlenecks, drop-offs, and areas for improvement. Use data-driven insights to refine your funnel and optimize the customer journey.

12. Adapt to Customer Feedback: Customer feedback is a goldmine of information. Listen to your customers, gather feedback, and use it to adapt your sales funnel to better align with their preferences and needs.

13. A/B Testing: Experiment with different approaches at each stage of the funnel. A/B testing can help you identify what works best for your specific audience, leading to more effective conversion strategies.

14. Mobile Optimization: Ensure that your sales funnel is mobile-friendly. Many potential customers access your SaaS product on their smartphones or tablets, so an optimized mobile experience is crucial.

15. Multichannel Engagement: Engage with prospects and customers across multiple channels. This includes email, social media, chat, and in-person interactions if applicable. Consistency in your messaging is key.

16. Customer Support: Post-conversion, provide exceptional customer support. Promptly address issues and inquiries to maintain customer satisfaction and loyalty.

17. Upselling and Cross-selling: Look for opportunities to upsell or cross-sell to existing customers. Offer additional features or complementary products that align with their needs.

18. Referral Programs: Encourage satisfied customers to refer others to your SaaS solution. Referral programs can be a powerful way to expand your customer base.

19. Continuously Monitor and Evolve: The SaaS industry is dynamic, with new trends and technologies emerging regularly. Keep an eye on industry developments and adjust your sales funnel accordingly to remain competitive.

In summary, creating an effective sales funnel in the SaaS industry is a dynamic and ongoing process. By understanding your target audience, providing value at each stage, and adapting to customer feedback, you can guide prospects from awareness to action, turning them into loyal customers. The success of your SaaS venture relies on the continual refinement of your sales funnel, ensuring it stays aligned with the ever-changing needs and preferences of your audience.

Customer Acquisition and Retention

Customer acquisition and retention are two sides of the same coin, each vital for the growth and sustainability of your SaaS business. In this chapter, we'll explore strategies and techniques to effectively acquire new customers and keep them engaged and loyal.

Customer Acquisition Strategies

Acquiring new customers is the lifeblood of any SaaS company. To fuel your growth, consider the following customer acquisition strategies:

1. Content Marketing: Create valuable, informative, and engaging content that addresses the pain points and needs of your target audience. This content can take the form of blog posts, ebooks, webinars, and videos. Use search engine optimization (SEO) to ensure your content is discoverable by your potential customers.

2. Social Media Marketing: Leverage social media platforms to connect with your audience. Share your content, engage in conversations, and utilize targeted advertising to reach potential customers who match your ideal customer persona.

3. Email Marketing: Develop personalized email campaigns that cater to the interests and preferences of your target audience. Segment your email list based on customer personas and behavioral data to send relevant messages.

4. Search Engine Marketing (SEM): Use paid advertising, such as Google Ads, to capture high-intent leads actively searching for solutions like yours. SEM can be an effective way to reach potential customers who are already interested in your niche.

5. Referral Programs: Encourage your existing customers to refer new customers to your SaaS solution. Implement a referral program that rewards both the referrer and the referee, motivating your current customer base to advocate for your product.

6. Partnerships and Alliances: Explore partnerships with companies that share your target audience. Joint marketing efforts and co-branded initiatives can expand your reach and bring in new leads.

7. Free Trials and Freemium Models: Offer free trials or freemium versions of your SaaS product to let potential customers experience its value firsthand. This can be an effective way to reduce the friction of trying out your solution.

8. Webinars and Demos: Host webinars and provide one-on-one demos to showcase your SaaS product's capabilities. These interactive sessions can engage potential customers and demonstrate the benefits of your solution.

9. Influencer Marketing: Collaborate with influencers in your industry to reach a wider audience. Influencers can vouch for your SaaS product, building trust with their followers.

10. Paid Advertising: Invest in online advertising, such as display ads or social media ads, to increase your brand visibility and attract potential customers. Pay-per-click (PPC) advertising allows you to control your budget and reach a specific audience.

11. Community Building: Create and nurture a community around your SaaS product. Engage with your target audience in forums, online groups, or social media communities. Actively participating in these spaces can generate interest and trust in your brand.

12. Web Presence Optimization: Optimize your website for conversion. This includes clear calls to action, user-friendly design, and landing pages that lead potential customers down the sales funnel.

Customer Retention Strategies

While customer acquisition is essential, customer retention is equally critical for the long-term success of your SaaS business. Retaining existing customers often proves more cost-effective than acquiring new ones. Here are strategies to foster customer retention:

1. Exceptional Customer Support: Provide top-notch customer support to address inquiries, issues, and concerns. Prompt and effective customer service fosters trust and loyalty.

2. Product Updates and Enhancements: Continuously improve your SaaS product by offering regular updates and enhancements. Keep your product fresh and aligned with the evolving needs of your customers.

3. Personalized Communication: Send personalized messages to customers based on their interaction with your product. Use data-driven insights to tailor your communications, offering relevant content and solutions.

4. Customer Onboarding: Create a seamless onboarding process for new customers. Guide them through the setup and initial use of your SaaS product to ensure they experience its value quickly.

5. Loyalty Programs: Develop loyalty programs that reward long-term customers. Offer exclusive benefits, discounts, or early access to new features as incentives for continued subscription.

6. Customer Feedback and Surveys: Regularly gather feedback from your customers. Use surveys and direct feedback to understand their pain points, expectations, and suggestions for improvement.

7. Churn Analysis: Analyze customer churn data to identify trends and common reasons for cancellation. Address these issues proactively to reduce churn rates.

8. Upselling and Cross-selling: Identify opportunities to upsell or cross-sell to existing customers. Offer additional features or complementary products that align with their needs and usage patterns.

9. Customer Education: Provide resources and content that educate your customers on how to make the most of your SaaS product. Webinars, tutorials, and guides can enhance their experience.

10. Customer Community: Foster a sense of community among your customers. Encourage interaction, knowledge sharing, and support among users. A strong customer community can enhance customer retention.

11. Proactive Outreach: Reach out to customers before they encounter issues. Proactive communication can identify potential problems and provide solutions before customers consider canceling their subscriptions.

12. Data Security and Compliance: Ensure that your SaaS product complies with data security and industry-specific regulations. Customer data security is a fundamental aspect of retaining trust.

13. Customer Success Teams: Establish dedicated customer success teams to work closely with your customers. These teams can provide ongoing guidance and support, ensuring customers achieve their goals using your product.

14. Retention Marketing: Develop marketing campaigns that specifically target existing customers. Promote additional services, features, or renewals to keep customers engaged and active.

15. Quality User Experience: Prioritize user experience in your product design. A user-friendly interface, fast loading times, and smooth navigation contribute to customer satisfaction.

16. Recognize and Reward: Acknowledge customer milestones, such as anniversaries with your product, and reward loyal customers with special offers or recognition.

17. Continuous Monitoring and Improvement: Continuously monitor customer retention metrics and identify areas for improvement. Be agile in adapting your strategies to meet changing customer needs.

18. Active Customer Listening: Actively listen to your customers' concerns and requests. Make changes based on their feedback, demonstrating that you value their opinions.

19. Data Analytics: Utilize data analytics to gain insights into customer behavior and preferences. This information can inform your retention strategies and help you anticipate customer needs.

Customer acquisition and retention are the twin pillars of a successful SaaS business. By implementing effective acquisition strategies, you can expand your customer base, while retention strategies nurture long-lasting customer relationships. The combination of both approaches is essential for sustainable growth and ensuring your SaaS venture thrives in a competitive landscape.

Chapter 6: SaaS Customer Support and Success

Providing Exceptional Customer Support

Exceptional customer support is the cornerstone of a thriving Software as a Service (SaaS) business. It's not just about addressing issues; it's about creating positive experiences, fostering trust, and retaining loyal customers. In this chapter, we'll delve into strategies and techniques for providing exceptional customer support in the SaaS industry.

Understanding the Importance of Customer Support

Before diving into the strategies for exceptional customer support, it's crucial to understand why it matters in the context of SaaS:

1. **Customer Retention**: Exceptional support plays a pivotal role in customer retention. When customers feel valued and well-supported, they are more likely to stay with your SaaS product and renew their subscriptions.

2. **Customer Loyalty**: Going above and beyond in providing support can lead to customer loyalty. Loyal customers are not only more likely to continue using your SaaS solution but also more likely to refer others to your product.

3. **Positive Reviews and Testimonials**: Exceptional support experiences often result in positive reviews and testimonials. These serve as social proof, influencing potential customers who are researching your product.

4. **Reduced Churn**: Effective support can reduce churn rates by addressing issues promptly and providing solutions to customer concerns, preventing cancellations.

5. **Brand Reputation**: High-quality support enhances your brand's reputation. Word-of-mouth recommendations and online reviews can significantly impact how your brand is perceived.

Strategies for Exceptional Customer Support

Now, let's explore strategies to provide exceptional customer support in the SaaS industry:

1. Multichannel Support: Offer support through multiple channels such as email, live chat, phone, and a self-service knowledge base. Different customers prefer different methods, so catering to their preferences is essential.

2. Swift Response Times: Respond to customer inquiries promptly. Time is of the essence, and quick responses show customers that you value their time and concerns.

3. 24/7 Availability: If possible, provide 24/7 support, especially if your SaaS product is used by customers in different time zones. This ensures assistance is available whenever customers need it.

4. Self-Service Resources: Create a comprehensive knowledge base that includes FAQs, tutorials, and guides. Many customers prefer to find solutions on their own, and a well-organized knowledge base can empower them to do so.

5. Personalization: Address customers by their names, and tailor your responses to their specific issues. Personalization makes customers feel valued and appreciated.

6. Training and Onboarding: Provide training and onboarding materials to help customers get the most out of your SaaS product. This is particularly important for new customers to ensure a smooth start.

7. Support Ticketing System: Implement a support ticketing system that allows customers to track the progress of their requests. Transparency in the support process builds trust.

8. Customer Feedback: Actively seek and act on customer feedback. Use surveys, feedback forms, and reviews to understand customer sentiments and make necessary improvements.

9. Empathetic Communication: Show empathy when dealing with customer issues. Understand their frustration, and communicate in a caring and compassionate manner.

10. Proactive Outreach: Anticipate customer needs by proactively reaching out to offer assistance. For example, if you notice a drop in usage, send a friendly inquiry to understand the issue.

11. Service Level Agreements (SLAs): Establish clear SLAs for response and resolution times. Communicate these to customers so they know what to expect in terms of support.

12. Escalation Path: Define an escalation path for complex issues. Ensure customers are aware of how to escalate their concerns if they feel their problem is not being adequately addressed.

13. Multilingual Support: If your customer base is international, consider offering support in multiple languages to accommodate diverse users.

14. Training and Continuous Learning: Invest in the training and continuous learning of your support team. Well-informed and skilled support agents can handle customer issues more effectively.

15. Integration with Customer Relationship Management (CRM) Systems: Integrate your support system with CRM systems to access customer information and history easily. This enables more personalized support.

16. Social Media Monitoring: Keep an eye on social media platforms for mentions of your brand or product. Address any negative comments or issues publicly to demonstrate your commitment to customer satisfaction.

17. Customer Support Metrics: Track key support metrics such as response times, resolution times, customer satisfaction scores, and churn rates. Data-driven insights can inform improvements.

18. Staffing Flexibility: Be prepared to adjust staffing levels during peak support times. Seasonal or event-driven fluctuations may require additional support agents.

19. Handling Customer Complaints: Develop a clear process for handling customer complaints. Ensure that issues are resolved to the customer's satisfaction and that the same problems do not recur.

20. Post-Support Follow-up: After resolving a customer's issue, follow up to ensure they are satisfied with the resolution. This shows that you care about their experience.

21. Data Security and Privacy: Ensure that customer data is handled with the utmost security and privacy. Assure customers that their data is safe with your SaaS product.

22. Chatbots and AI: Implement chatbots and artificial intelligence (AI) for routine inquiries and support ticket creation. These technologies can expedite support and provide instant responses.

23. Customer Advocacy Programs: Establish customer advocacy programs to reward and recognize loyal customers. Advocate customers can become brand ambassadors.

24. Service Recovery: When a mistake occurs, own up to it, and take steps to rectify the situation. How you handle errors can significantly impact customer trust.

25. Regular Training Updates: Keep your support team updated on the latest product features and changes. This ensures they can provide accurate and helpful assistance.

Providing exceptional customer support is not merely a necessity; it's a powerful way to differentiate your SaaS business in a competitive landscape. By offering a range of support options, personalizing interactions, and being responsive and empathetic, you can create a loyal customer base that not only sticks around but also becomes advocates for your brand. Remember that customer support is an ongoing commitment, and continuous improvement is essential to meet the evolving needs of your customers.

Onboarding and Training Customers

In the dynamic world of Software as a Service (SaaS), the initial experience a customer has with your product can greatly influence their long-term success and satisfaction. To ensure customers maximize the value of your SaaS solution, a well-planned onboarding and training process is crucial. In this chapter, we will explore the strategies and methods for effectively onboarding and training SaaS customers.

The Significance of Onboarding and Training

Before we delve into the strategies and techniques, it's important to understand why onboarding and training are of utmost importance in the SaaS industry:

1. **Product Adoption**: Effective onboarding and training accelerate product adoption. When customers understand how to use your SaaS product, they are more likely to integrate it into their workflow.

2. **Customer Satisfaction**: A smooth onboarding experience and comprehensive training build customer satisfaction. Satisfied customers are more likely to stay with your product and renew their subscriptions.

3. **Reduced Churn**: By helping customers get started and achieve their goals with your SaaS product, you can reduce churn rates. Customers are less likely to cancel their subscriptions when they're successfully using your product.

4. **Product Understanding**: Onboarding and training ensure that customers fully comprehend the capabilities and features of your SaaS solution. This leads to more effective usage and increased value.

5. **Customer Success**: Onboarding and training are essential components of the broader customer success strategy. When customers succeed with your product, they are more likely to become advocates and refer others.

Strategies for Effective Onboarding

Effective onboarding is a step-by-step process that introduces customers to your SaaS product and guides them through initial setup and usage. Consider the following strategies:

1. **Personalized Onboarding**: Tailor the onboarding process to the specific needs of individual customers. Use the data you've collected during the sales and sign-up process to create customized onboarding paths.

2. **Welcome Emails**: Send a personalized welcome email to new customers. This email should introduce them to your product and provide links to resources for getting started.

3. **Product Tours**: Offer guided product tours that showcase key features and functionalities. These tours can help customers understand the core capabilities of your SaaS solution.

4. **Video Tutorials**: Create video tutorials that demonstrate how to use your product effectively. Videos are an engaging way to convey information and can be accessed at the customer's convenience.

5. **Self-Service Guides**: Develop self-service guides, FAQs, and documentation that customers can access when they have questions or need assistance. Organize this information in an easy-to-navigate format.

6. **User Guides and Documentation**: Provide in-depth user guides and documentation for those who prefer a detailed, written reference. These guides should cover all aspects of using your SaaS product.

7. **Interactive Demos**: Offer interactive demos that allow customers to try out different features of your product. This hands-on experience can be particularly effective in helping customers understand how your SaaS solution works.

8. **Checklists**: Create onboarding checklists that customers can follow. Checklists help customers keep track of their progress and ensure they complete essential setup steps.

9. **Live Webinars**: Host live webinars or online training sessions to engage with customers in real-time. Webinars enable customers to ask questions and receive immediate responses.

10. **Customer Support During Onboarding**: Ensure that customer support is readily available during the onboarding process. If customers encounter issues, they should be able to access assistance quickly.

11. **Feedback Collection**: Collect feedback from customers during and after the onboarding process. Use this feedback to refine your onboarding process and address any shortcomings.

12. **Gamification**: Gamify the onboarding process by offering rewards or badges for completing certain steps. Gamification can make onboarding more engaging and enjoyable.

13. **Progress Tracking**: Allow customers to track their progress during onboarding. Clearly indicate what steps they've completed and what remains to be done.

Strategies for Effective Customer Training

Beyond the onboarding process, training customers is an ongoing effort to ensure they make the most of your SaaS product. Here are strategies for effective customer training:

1. **Modular Training**: Offer training in a modular format, allowing customers to focus on the specific areas or features they need. This makes training more targeted and efficient.

2. **Role-Based Training**: Provide training that is tailored to different user roles within an organization. Administrators, managers, and end-users may have distinct training needs.

3. **Advanced Training**: Offer advanced training for customers who want to explore more complex features and capabilities of your SaaS product.

4. **Certification Programs**: Create certification programs that customers can complete to demonstrate their proficiency with your product. Certifications can add value to their resumes.

5. **Regular Training Webinars**: Host regular training webinars and workshops to keep customers informed about new features and best practices. These sessions can also serve as opportunities for interaction.

6. **In-App Help and Tooltips**: Incorporate in-app help and tooltips that guide users through features as they interact with your SaaS product. This provides real-time assistance.

7. **Knowledge Base Updates**: Maintain an up-to-date knowledge base that covers both basic and advanced usage of your product. Ensure that this resource reflects the latest changes and updates.

8. **User Forums and Communities**: Foster user forums and communities where customers can discuss their experiences and share insights. These platforms can serve as valuable training resources.

9. **User Workshops**: Organize workshops where customers can collaborate and learn from each other. These interactive sessions can provide unique training opportunities.

10. **Subscription Plans with Training**: Offer subscription plans that include training as part of the package. This incentivizes customers to engage in training and continuously improve their skills.

11. **Feedback and Q&A Sessions**: Schedule regular feedback and Q&A sessions where customers can provide input and ask questions. These sessions can be valuable for addressing specific training needs.

12. **Mobile-Friendly Training**: Ensure that training materials are accessible on mobile devices, as many customers may prefer to learn on their smartphones or tablets.

13. **Customer Success Managers**: Assign customer success managers to provide ongoing support and training. These managers can work closely with customers to understand their needs and offer personalized training.

14. **Performance Analytics**: Track customer performance and product usage. Use this data to identify areas where additional training may be required and to personalize training plans.

15. **Integration with CRM**: Integrate training data with customer relationship management (CRM) systems to maintain a record of customer progress and training history.

User Feedback and Iteration

An essential aspect of both onboarding and training is collecting user feedback and using it to iterate and improve the process. Regularly solicit feedback from customers and use this information to enhance your onboarding and training programs. Make adjustments based on customer input to ensure that the training process remains relevant and effective.

In summary, effective onboarding and training are vital components of a successful SaaS customer support and success strategy. By providing personalized onboarding experiences and comprehensive training resources, you can help customers unlock the full potential of your SaaS product. These efforts contribute to customer satisfaction, retention, and advocacy, ensuring your SaaS business thrives in a competitive market.

Measuring and Improving Customer Success

Customer success is the lifeblood of a Software as a Service (SaaS) business. It's not merely about acquiring customers but ensuring that they achieve their goals and derive value from your product. To do this effectively, you must measure and continuously improve customer success. In this chapter, we explore the strategies and techniques for assessing and enhancing customer success in the SaaS industry.

The Significance of Measuring and Improving Customer Success

Before diving into the strategies for measuring and improving customer success, it's important to understand why this is of paramount importance in the SaaS industry:

1. **Customer Retention**: Measuring and improving customer success are closely linked to customer retention. Customers who succeed with your product are more likely to continue using it and renew their subscriptions.

2. **Customer Advocacy**: Satisfied, successful customers often become advocates for your SaaS product. They refer others, share positive experiences, and contribute to your brand's reputation.

3. **Reduced Churn**: By identifying and addressing factors that impede customer success, you can reduce churn rates. Understanding why customers leave and making improvements can help retain more customers.

4. **Product Development**: Customer success insights inform product development. Understanding how customers use your product and what problems they encounter allows you to refine your offering.

5. **Competitive Advantage**: High levels of customer success give your SaaS business a competitive edge. Happy, successful customers are less likely to explore alternatives, even if they exist.

Strategies for Measuring Customer Success

To measure customer success, you must define the metrics and Key Performance Indicators (KPIs) that are relevant to your SaaS business. Here are strategies to effectively measure customer success:

1. Define Clear Objectives: Establish clear, measurable objectives that define customer success. What are the specific goals that customers should achieve using your SaaS product?

2. Customer Surveys: Implement regular customer surveys to gather feedback and insights. Ask customers to rate their satisfaction, the value they derive from your product, and their likelihood to recommend it.

3. Net Promoter Score (NPS): Calculate the Net Promoter Score, which measures customer loyalty and willingness to recommend your product. NPS surveys are simple and effective.

4. Customer Health Scores: Develop a customer health scoring system to assess the overall health of your customer relationships. Consider factors such as product usage, engagement, and feedback.

5. Customer Lifetime Value (CLV): Calculate the CLV of your customers to determine their long-term value to your business. Higher CLV indicates greater customer success and retention.

6. Churn Rate: Monitor your churn rate to understand how many customers are leaving your SaaS product. Identifying reasons for churn is critical for improving customer success.

7. Feature Adoption: Analyze which product features or functionalities customers use most frequently. High feature adoption rates are indicators of successful product usage.

8. Customer Support Metrics: Track customer support metrics such as response times, resolution times, and customer satisfaction scores. These metrics reflect the effectiveness of your support efforts.

9. User Engagement Metrics: Assess user engagement metrics, including logins, click-through rates, and time spent using your SaaS product. Engaged users are more likely to be successful customers.

10. Expansion Revenue: Measure expansion revenue generated from upsells, cross-sells, and renewals. Expansion revenue is a clear indication of customer success and loyalty.

11. Customer Feedback Analysis: Analyze feedback from customers to understand their pain points, needs, and suggestions. Feedback analysis can uncover areas for improvement.

12. Product Usage Patterns: Study how customers use your SaaS product. Analyze user behavior to identify usage patterns that indicate successful or struggling customers.

13. Case Studies and Success Stories: Share case studies and success stories of customers who have achieved significant success using your product. These stories serve as examples of what's possible.

14. Post-Interaction Surveys: After customer interactions with support or training, conduct brief surveys to gauge customer satisfaction and identify areas for improvement.

Strategies for Improving Customer Success

Once you've measured customer success, the next step is to implement strategies for continuous improvement. Here are strategies for enhancing customer success:

1. Proactive Outreach: Reach out to customers proactively to offer assistance and address any issues they may encounter. Identifying and resolving problems in a timely manner can boost customer success.

2. Personalized Recommendations: Provide personalized recommendations to customers based on their usage patterns and needs. Help them discover how to get more value from your product.

3. Customer Success Managers: Assign customer success managers to work closely with customers. These managers can understand customer goals, identify potential challenges, and offer personalized guidance.

4. Ongoing Training: Offer ongoing training and resources to help customers continually improve their skills and understanding of your product. Regular training sessions and webinars can be effective.

5. Customer Advocacy Programs: Develop customer advocacy programs that recognize and reward loyal, successful customers. Advocate customers can become brand ambassadors.

6. Feature Updates and Enhancements: Continuously improve your product based on customer feedback and changing market needs. Regular feature updates and enhancements can make your product more valuable.

7. Customer Forums and Communities: Foster customer forums and communities where customers can share experiences, insights, and best practices. These platforms can be valuable for self-help and knowledge sharing.

8. User Workshops: Organize user workshops where customers can collaborate and learn from each other. These interactive sessions provide unique training opportunities and encourage sharing of success stories.

9. Regular Customer Success Reviews: Conduct regular customer success reviews with key accounts. Discuss their goals, challenges, and strategies for achieving success with your product.

10. Case Studies and Success Stories: Share more case studies and success stories to inspire other customers and help them see the possibilities with your product.

11. Churn Analysis and Recovery: Regularly analyze churn data to identify trends and common reasons for cancellation. Address these issues proactively to reduce churn rates and recover lost customers.

12. Product Documentation Updates: Keep your product documentation up-to-date and easily accessible. Documentation should reflect the latest changes and provide guidance for successful usage.

13. Continuous Training Updates: Keep your training materials updated to align with product updates and evolving customer needs. Training should be relevant and responsive to changes.

14. Integration with CRM Systems: Integrate customer success data with CRM systems to maintain a comprehensive record of customer interactions and progress.

15. Mobile-Friendly Resources: Ensure that training and resources are accessible on mobile devices. Customers often prefer to access information on smartphones or tablets.

16. Post-Support Follow-up: After resolving a customer's support issue, follow up to ensure they are satisfied with the resolution. This additional step demonstrates your commitment to their success.

Measuring and improving customer success are essential components of a thriving SaaS business. By monitoring customer metrics, implementing strategies for ongoing improvement, and fostering a culture of customer success, you can create a loyal customer base that not only sticks around but also becomes advocates for your brand. This approach ensures your SaaS venture thrives in a competitive market and continues to meet the evolving needs of your customers.

Chapter 7: SaaS Security and Data Privacy

Protecting Customer Data

In the realm of Software as a Service (SaaS), the security and privacy of customer data are paramount. Customers trust SaaS providers to safeguard their sensitive information, and any breach or mishandling of data can lead to severe consequences. This chapter explores the critical aspects of protecting customer data in the context of SaaS, including security measures, compliance, and best practices.

Data Security Measures

1. **Data Encryption:** Implement strong encryption mechanisms to protect data both in transit and at rest. Secure Sockets Layer (SSL)/Transport Layer Security (TLS) protocols should be used for data in transit, while data at rest should be encrypted using encryption algorithms like Advanced Encryption Standard (AES).

2. **Access Controls:** Restrict access to customer data by enforcing strong authentication, authorization, and access control policies. Only authorized personnel should have access to sensitive data, and role-based access controls can help manage permissions effectively.

3. **Authentication Methods:** Utilize multi-factor authentication (MFA) for added security. MFA requires users to provide two or more forms of verification before accessing their data, making it more challenging for unauthorized individuals to gain access.

4. **Data Backup and Recovery:** Regularly back up customer data and establish disaster recovery procedures to ensure data availability in the event of data loss, natural disasters, or system failures.

5. **Security Patch Management:** Stay up to date with security patches for the software and systems used in your SaaS platform. Regularly apply updates to address vulnerabilities and security issues.

6. **Security Audits and Testing:** Conduct regular security audits and penetration testing to identify vulnerabilities and weaknesses in your SaaS infrastructure. Address any issues promptly to strengthen your security posture.

Data Privacy Compliance

1. **Data Protection Regulations:** Familiarize yourself with data protection regulations relevant to your operating regions. For example, the General Data Protection Regulation (GDPR) in Europe, the Health Insurance Portability and Accountability Act (HIPAA) in the United States, or the Personal Data Protection Act (PDPA) in Singapore.

2. **Data Mapping:** Understand the flow of customer data within your SaaS platform. Create a data map that identifies how data is collected, processed, stored, and deleted.

3. **Data Privacy Policies:** Develop clear and comprehensive data privacy policies and ensure they are easily accessible to your customers. These policies should outline how you handle customer data, including data retention, deletion, and disclosure practices.

4. **Consent Management:** Implement robust consent management processes to obtain and record user consent for data processing. Ensure that users have a clear understanding of what they are consenting to.

5. **Data Minimization:** Adopt a data minimization approach, collecting only the data necessary for the intended purpose. Avoid the unnecessary collection and storage of customer data.

6. **Data Portability:** Enable customers to access and export their data in a structured and machine-readable format. This ensures data portability and empowers users to switch to alternative services.

Best Practices for Protecting Customer Data

1. **Employee Training:** Train your employees on data security best practices and data privacy regulations. Ensure they understand the importance of safeguarding customer data.

2. **Incident Response Plan:** Develop a well-defined incident response plan that outlines how to handle data breaches or security incidents. This plan should include steps for notification, remediation, and communication with affected customers.

3. **Vendor Management:** If you use third-party services or vendors, ensure they have robust security measures in place and comply with data privacy regulations. Implement vendor risk management processes to assess and monitor their security practices.

4. **Data Encryption in Transit and At Rest:** Implement encryption for data transmission and storage. Utilize strong encryption algorithms and protocols to protect customer data.

5. **Regular Security Audits:** Conduct regular security audits and assessments of your SaaS platform. Engage with security experts to identify vulnerabilities and areas for improvement.

6. **Customer Education:** Educate your customers about data security and privacy practices. Provide them with resources and information on how they can protect their data when using your SaaS product.

Transparency and Communication

1. **Privacy Policy:** Maintain a comprehensive and up-to-date privacy policy that clearly explains how you handle customer data. Make it easily accessible on your website and within your SaaS platform.

2. **Data Breach Notifications:** In the event of a data breach, notify affected customers promptly, providing clear and transparent information about the breach, its impact, and the actions being taken to address it.

3. **Customer Support:** Offer responsive and accessible customer support channels for data-related inquiries and concerns. Ensure that customers can easily reach out for assistance.

4. **Compliance Reporting:** If applicable, report your data privacy compliance status and adherence to regulations, which can build trust with your customers.

Conclusion

Protecting customer data in the SaaS industry is not just a legal obligation; it's a moral imperative. By implementing robust security measures, complying with data privacy regulations, and following best practices, SaaS providers can create a secure environment where customer data is safeguarded. Transparency and open communication further enhance trust and confidence in the platform. In the next chapter, we'll explore disaster recovery and business continuity strategies to ensure the resilience of your SaaS services.

Regulatory Compliance

Numerous regulations and standards govern the collection, storage, and processing of customer data, requiring SaaS providers to adhere to strict guidelines to protect user privacy and security. This chapter delves into two prominent regulatory frameworks, the General Data Protection Regulation (GDPR) and the Health Insurance Portability and Accountability Act (HIPAA), and outlines the essential steps SaaS providers must take to achieve compliance.

General Data Protection Regulation (GDPR)

The GDPR is a comprehensive data protection regulation enacted by the European Union (EU) in 2018. It is designed to protect the privacy and personal data of EU citizens, regardless of where that data is processed. GDPR compliance is a vital consideration for SaaS providers, even if they are not physically located in the EU, as it impacts any organization handling data of EU residents.

Key Aspects of GDPR Compliance

1. **Data Mapping:** Understand how customer data flows through your SaaS platform. Create a data map that outlines data collection, processing, storage, and deletion processes.

2. **Data Protection Impact Assessment (DPIA):** Conduct DPIAs for high-risk data processing activities. This assessment helps identify and mitigate risks to data subjects' privacy.

3. **Data Privacy Policies:** Develop and maintain clear data privacy policies that explain how you handle customer data, including data retention, deletion, and disclosure practices.

4. **Consent Management:** Implement strong consent management processes to obtain and record user consent for data processing. Consent must be freely given, specific, informed, and unambiguous.

5. **Data Portability:** Allow customers to access and export their data in a structured, machine-readable format. This empowers users to move their data to alternative services.

6. **Right to Be Forgotten:** Enable customers to request the deletion of their data, following GDPR guidelines for erasure. This may involve data pseudonymization or anonymization to maintain data integrity.

7. **Data Breach Notification:** Establish clear procedures for reporting data breaches to relevant authorities and affected customers. Timely notifications are a key component of GDPR compliance.

Health Insurance Portability and Accountability Act (HIPAA)

HIPAA is a United States federal law enacted in 1996 to safeguard the privacy and security of individuals' medical information. It primarily affects SaaS providers operating in the healthcare industry. HIPAA compliance is vital for SaaS platforms that process or store protected health information (PHI).

Key Aspects of HIPAA Compliance

1. **Data Encryption:** Encrypt all data at rest and in transit to protect the confidentiality and integrity of PHI.

2. **Access Control:** Implement strict access controls, ensuring that only authorized personnel can access PHI. Role-based access control is a common practice.

3. **Audit Trails:** Maintain detailed audit trails to monitor access to PHI. This helps track and investigate potential security incidents.

4. **Business Associate Agreements (BAAs):** Sign BAAs with any third-party service providers who have access to PHI. These agreements establish responsibility for HIPAA compliance.

5. **Security Risk Assessment:** Regularly conduct security risk assessments to identify vulnerabilities and mitigate security risks to PHI.

6. **Training:** Train employees on HIPAA regulations, security best practices, and the importance of protecting PHI.

7. **Incident Response Plan:** Develop an incident response plan for addressing security breaches or unauthorized disclosures of PHI. Ensure that this plan includes the necessary steps for breach notification.

Best Practices for Regulatory Compliance

1. **Understand Applicability:** Thoroughly understand which regulations are applicable to your SaaS platform based on your user base and data processing activities.

2. **Data Protection Officer (DPO):** Appoint a Data Protection Officer or a responsible individual who oversees compliance and ensures that all necessary measures are in place.

3. **Privacy by Design:** Incorporate privacy considerations into the design and development of your SaaS product. Data protection should be an integral part of the development process.

4. **Regular Audits:** Conduct regular compliance audits and assessments to identify any areas of non-compliance and address them promptly.

5. **Customer Education:** Educate your customers about their responsibilities in using your SaaS product while adhering to relevant regulations. Offer guidance and resources to support their compliance.

6. **Transparency:** Maintain transparent communication with your customers about your compliance efforts. Make your data privacy policies and practices easily accessible.

Compliance Reporting

1. **Data Protection Impact Assessment (DPIA):** Record and maintain DPIAs for high-risk data processing activities.

2. **Incident Reports:** Document and report all data breaches and security incidents, along with the actions taken to mitigate and rectify them.

3. **Regulatory Reporting:** If a regulatory authority requires reporting or auditing, ensure that you promptly comply with their requests.

Regulatory compliance is a fundamental responsibility for SaaS providers, and non-compliance can lead to significant legal and financial consequences. By thoroughly understanding and adhering to regulations such as GDPR and HIPAA, implementing security measures, and educating both employees and customers, SaaS providers can create a trustworthy and secure environment for data processing. In the next chapter, we'll explore disaster recovery and business continuity strategies to ensure the resilience of your SaaS services in the face of unforeseen events.

Responding to Security Threats

In the world of Software as a Service (SaaS), security threats are a constant concern. SaaS providers face an array of potential risks, from data breaches to cyberattacks. Responding effectively to these threats is essential to safeguard customer data, maintain business continuity, and protect your reputation. This chapter outlines key strategies and best practices for responding to security threats in the context of SaaS.

Security Threats in SaaS

1. **Data Breaches:** Data breaches occur when unauthorized individuals gain access to sensitive customer data. These breaches can result from various factors, including weak passwords, insider threats, or external attacks.

2. **Cyberattacks:** Cyberattacks encompass a wide range of malicious activities, such as ransomware attacks, Distributed Denial of Service (DDoS) attacks, and malware infections, which aim to disrupt services or compromise data.

3. **Phishing:** Phishing attacks involve fraudulent emails or messages that trick users into revealing sensitive information, such as login credentials or personal details.

4. **Insider Threats:** Insider threats can be intentional or unintentional. They occur when individuals within the organization misuse their access to compromise security.

5. **Third-Party Vulnerabilities:** Security vulnerabilities in third-party integrations or services used by the SaaS platform can pose risks if not properly managed.

Effective Response to Security Threats

1. **Incident Response Plan:** Develop a well-defined incident response plan that outlines the steps to take when a security threat is detected. This plan should include roles and responsibilities, communication procedures, and a clear escalation process.

2. **Security Incident Detection:** Implement robust security incident detection mechanisms. Utilize intrusion detection systems (IDS), intrusion prevention systems (IPS), and Security Information and Event Management (SIEM) tools to monitor for suspicious activities.

3. **Notification and Communication:** Establish clear communication protocols for informing relevant stakeholders about security incidents. This includes notifying customers, law enforcement, regulatory bodies, and affected third parties.

4. **Data Preservation:** When a security threat is detected, preserve all relevant data and logs for forensic analysis. This is crucial for understanding the scope and impact of the incident.

5. **Containment and Mitigation:** Act promptly to contain the security threat to prevent further damage. Isolate compromised systems, block malicious traffic, and mitigate vulnerabilities.

6. **Forensic Analysis:** Conduct a thorough forensic analysis to understand the nature and source of the security threat. This analysis helps in making informed decisions and preventing future incidents.

Customer Communication

1. **Transparency:** Be transparent with customers about the security incident. Provide clear and concise information about what occurred, the potential impact, and the steps taken to address the threat.

2. **Notification Timeliness:** Notify customers promptly after confirming a security incident. Delayed notifications can erode trust and allow customers to take preventive measures.

3. **Assistance and Support:** Offer customers guidance on protecting their data and systems in the aftermath of the incident. Provide support and resources to help them navigate the situation.

4. **Update Communication:** Keep customers informed throughout the incident response process. Regular updates on progress and outcomes demonstrate your commitment to resolution.

Legal and Regulatory Obligations

1. **Regulatory Reporting:** If the security incident involves customer data, report it to relevant regulatory authorities as required by data protection regulations. Compliance with such obligations is essential.

2. **Contractual Obligations:** Review your contractual agreements with customers to understand any obligations or liabilities related to security incidents. Be prepared to meet these obligations.

3. **Litigation and Liability:** Be aware of potential legal liabilities stemming from security incidents. Consult legal counsel to navigate any legal issues, including potential lawsuits.

Continuous Improvement

1. **Post-Incident Review:** Conduct a post-incident review to analyze the response process and identify areas for improvement. Use this information to refine your incident response plan.

2. **Training and Awareness:** Regularly train employees on security best practices and incident response procedures. Create a culture of security awareness within your organization.

3. **Threat Intelligence:** Stay informed about emerging threats and security trends. Utilize threat intelligence to enhance your security measures and response capabilities.

4. **Vulnerability Management:** Continuously monitor and address vulnerabilities in your SaaS platform. Regularly patch and update systems to minimize the risk of future incidents.

Collaboration and Sharing

1. **Information Sharing:** Collaborate with other SaaS providers and industry peers to share information about emerging threats and vulnerabilities. This collective approach strengthens the industry's security posture.

2. **External Support:** When necessary, seek external support from cybersecurity experts, law enforcement agencies, and incident response teams to address complex security threats.

3. **User Feedback:** Encourage customers to report any suspicious activities or security concerns they encounter. User feedback can be a valuable source of threat intelligence.

Security threats are a constant concern in the SaaS industry, and a swift and effective response is crucial to safeguard customer data and maintain trust. By developing a robust incident response plan, implementing strong detection mechanisms, and being transparent in communication with customers, SaaS providers can minimize the impact of security incidents. Continuous improvement, collaboration, and a commitment to security awareness are essential for enhancing the resilience of your SaaS platform. In the next chapter, we'll explore data backup, disaster recovery, and business continuity strategies to ensure the reliability and availability of your SaaS services.

Chapter 8: Scaling Your SaaS Business

Growing Your User Base

Expanding your SaaS business is an ongoing journey. As your software matures and your reputation solidifies, the natural next step is to grow your user base. This chapter explores strategies and best practices for attracting more customers, retaining them, and maximizing your growth potential.

1. Market Research and Targeting

Before scaling your user base, a deeper understanding of your market is essential. Conduct thorough market research to identify your ideal customer profile. This should include demographics, industry verticals, and pain points your SaaS solution addresses. Targeting the right audience is the foundation for successful growth.

2. User Onboarding

A smooth and intuitive onboarding process is crucial for new users. Make the initial experience as user-friendly as possible. Ensure your product provides value from the moment users sign up. Consider guided tours, tutorials, and well-designed interfaces to reduce barriers to entry.

3. Customer Support

Prompt and effective customer support is a linchpin of user retention. Happy customers are more likely to stay and recommend your service to others. Invest in a knowledgeable support team and responsive communication channels to address user concerns swiftly.

4. Pricing Strategies

Pricing can significantly impact user acquisition and retention. Experiment with various pricing models, such as freemium, tiered, or pay-as-you-go, to find what resonates with your target audience. Adjust pricing based on user feedback and market trends.

5. Referral Programs

Leveraging your existing user base can be a powerful growth strategy. Implement referral programs that reward current users for bringing in new customers. This taps into the trust your existing users have and can create a viral effect, expanding your user base organically.

6. Content Marketing

Creating and sharing valuable content establishes your SaaS business as an authority in your niche. Invest in a content marketing strategy that includes blog posts, whitepapers, webinars, and videos. High-quality content not only attracts users but also keeps them engaged.

7. SEO and SEM

Search engine optimization (SEO) and search engine marketing (SEM) are essential for reaching a broader audience. Optimize your website and content for relevant keywords. Use targeted paid advertising to get your SaaS solution in front of potential users actively searching for your type of software.

8. Social Media Marketing

Social media is a dynamic platform for connecting with your target audience. Use platforms like Twitter, LinkedIn, and Facebook to engage with potential users. Share your content, offer promotions, and create a community around your SaaS product.

9. Partnering and Integration

Collaborating with other SaaS providers can open up new growth opportunities. Partnerships and integrations with complementary software solutions can expand your reach and make your product more attractive to potential users.

10. User Feedback and Iteration

Listening to user feedback is a valuable growth tool. Actively collect and analyze feedback to improve your product continuously. Iterate on features, user interface, and functionality based on user needs and preferences.

11. Analytics and Data-Driven Decisions

Utilize analytics tools to gain insights into user behavior. Track key performance indicators (KPIs) to understand what drives user engagement and conversion. Data-driven decisions enable you to allocate resources effectively and make informed improvements.

12. User Training and Resources

Empower users with resources to get the most out of your product. Provide comprehensive documentation, video tutorials, and webinars. Well-informed users are more likely to remain loyal and advocate for your software.

13. Customer Retention

Retention is just as important as acquisition. Implement strategies to reduce churn, such as automated email campaigns, personalized recommendations, and loyalty programs.

14. Localization and Global Expansion

As your SaaS business grows, consider expanding to new markets. Localization, including translating your product and marketing materials, can help you tap into a global user base.

15. Scalability and Infrastructure

Ensure your infrastructure can handle the influx of new users. Scalability is vital to accommodate growth without compromising performance. Cloud solutions can provide the elasticity needed to scale efficiently.

16. Data Security and Privacy Compliance

With more users come increased responsibilities for data security and privacy. Ensure your SaaS solution complies with relevant data protection regulations. Security breaches can be detrimental to your growth efforts.

17. User Communities

Building user communities, such as forums or online groups, fosters engagement and loyalty. Users can share experiences, offer support, and provide insights that improve your product.

18. A/B Testing

Experiment with different approaches to understand what resonates with your target audience. A/B testing allows you to fine-tune your marketing messages and user interface to improve conversion rates.

19. User Surveys and Feedback Loops

Regularly survey your users to gain insights into their needs and preferences. Feedback loops are invaluable for understanding what's working and what needs improvement.

20. Continuous Innovation

To sustain growth, innovation must be ongoing. Stay ahead of the competition by developing new features, exploring emerging technologies, and adapting to the evolving needs of your user base.

In the competitive world of SaaS, growing your user base is a continuous journey. By strategically targeting your market, prioritizing user experience, and continually refining your approach, your SaaS business can thrive and achieve sustainable growth.

Infrastructure Scaling Strategies

When scaling your SaaS business, infrastructure is the backbone that supports your growth. To meet increased demand and maintain a seamless user experience, you need a robust infrastructure scaling strategy. In this chapter, we explore strategies to ensure your infrastructure can handle the demands of a growing user base.

1. Cloud Computing

Embracing cloud computing is a foundational step in ensuring scalable infrastructure. Cloud providers offer flexibility, scalability, and reliability that can be critical during periods of rapid growth. Whether you choose Amazon Web Services (AWS), Microsoft Azure, or Google Cloud Platform, cloud services allow you to scale your infrastructure resources as needed.

2. Load Balancing

Load balancing is a crucial element of scaling your infrastructure. Distributing incoming network traffic across multiple servers or data centers ensures that no single server is overloaded, leading to better performance and availability.

3. Auto-Scaling

Auto-scaling is a game-changer when it comes to managing fluctuating workloads. With auto-scaling, your infrastructure can automatically increase or decrease resources based on traffic, helping you save on costs during periods of low demand and ensuring sufficient resources during spikes.

4. Containerization

Containerization, often with Docker and Kubernetes, allows you to package and deploy applications consistently and efficiently across different environments. This approach enhances flexibility, making it easier to scale horizontally by adding more containers as needed.

5. Microservices Architecture

Breaking your application into smaller, independently deployable services is a strategic choice for scaling. Microservices enable you to scale specific components of your application independently, resulting in more efficient resource allocation.

6. Content Delivery Networks (CDNs)

CDNs are indispensable for improving the speed and reliability of content delivery. By caching and distributing content across a network of servers, CDNs reduce latency and deliver a better user experience, especially for users located far from your data centers.

7. Serverless Computing

Serverless computing, exemplified by AWS Lambda and Azure Functions, allows you to focus on writing code without managing the underlying infrastructure. It's an excellent choice for specific workloads and can help reduce operational overhead.

8. Data Sharding

Data sharding is a database optimization technique that involves splitting a database into smaller, more manageable parts called shards. This can significantly enhance the scalability of data storage and retrieval.

9. Global Data Centers

To ensure low-latency access for users worldwide, consider establishing data centers in different geographic regions. This approach helps maintain performance and offers redundancy in case of data center outages.

10. Data Caching

Caching frequently accessed data in memory can reduce the load on your database and improve response times. Utilize caching systems like Redis or Memcached to optimize data retrieval.

11. Content Optimization

Optimize the content and media files delivered to users. This includes compressing images and using appropriate file formats to reduce data transfer and improve page load times.

12. Continuous Monitoring and Performance Tuning

Implement robust monitoring tools to keep a close eye on your infrastructure's performance. Monitor key metrics, such as CPU usage, memory, and network activity. Regularly fine-tune your infrastructure based on data-driven insights.

13. Disaster Recovery Planning

Scaling doesn't just mean accommodating growth; it also involves preparing for unforeseen events. Develop a robust disaster recovery plan that includes backups, redundancy, and data recovery strategies to ensure minimal downtime in the event of a disaster.

14. Network Optimization

Ensure that your network infrastructure is optimized for efficient data transfer. High-speed connections, content distribution, and routing strategies are vital for delivering a smooth user experience.

15. Security and Compliance

Scalability should not compromise security. Implement robust security measures to protect your infrastructure. Regularly audit your security controls to ensure compliance with industry standards and regulations.

16. Traffic Analysis

Analyze traffic patterns to predict and prepare for surges in demand. Historical data and analytics can help you anticipate when and where scaling will be needed.

17. Database Scaling

Scaling databases is a significant challenge. Explore options such as vertical scaling (adding more resources to a single server) and horizontal scaling (adding more database servers). Choose the method that aligns with your data storage needs.

18. Capacity Planning

Maintain a proactive approach to capacity planning. Regularly assess your infrastructure's performance and usage trends to identify when additional resources or scaling is necessary.

19. DevOps Practices

Implement DevOps practices to streamline the development and deployment of infrastructure changes. Automation, continuous integration, and continuous delivery (CI/CD) pipelines can expedite the deployment of updates and new features.

20. Green Computing

Consider the environmental impact of your infrastructure. Green computing practices, such as using energy-efficient servers and data center designs, align with sustainability goals while also helping reduce operational costs.

SaaS business growth depends on scalable infrastructure. These strategies ensure your infrastructure can adapt to increased demand while maintaining the performance and reliability your users expect. Keep evolving and optimizing your infrastructure to meet the needs of a growing user base and the ever-changing technology landscape.

International Expansion

Expanding your SaaS business beyond your local market is a critical step for sustainable growth. International expansion broadens your user base, revenue streams, and global footprint. This chapter explores strategies and considerations for taking your SaaS business to the international stage.

1. Market Research

Before embarking on international expansion, comprehensive market research is a must. Analyze potential target markets to understand the competitive landscape, user demographics, and specific challenges and opportunities. Your SaaS product may need localization, customization, or adaptations to succeed in a new market.

2. Legal and Regulatory Compliance

Complying with international regulations is crucial. Different countries have various legal and compliance requirements, including data privacy regulations and business licensing. Consult with legal experts to ensure your SaaS business aligns with local laws and standards.

3. Cultural Sensitivity

Cultural differences can significantly impact your success in a new market. Adapt your marketing, user interface, and content to respect local customs and sensibilities. This demonstrates cultural sensitivity and makes your product more appealing to potential users.

4. Language Localization

Localizing your SaaS product means more than just translation. It involves adapting content, features, and user experience to match the language and cultural norms of your target audience. Professional translation services and native-speaking employees can help ensure effective localization.

5. Market Entry Strategies

Consider various market entry strategies, such as joint ventures, partnerships, or acquisitions, depending on your resources and market conditions. Alternatively, start by offering your SaaS product on a trial basis or through a soft launch to gauge user response and adjust your strategy accordingly.

6. International Customer Support

Providing customer support in the local language and time zone is essential. Efficient support is crucial for user satisfaction and building trust in a new market. Consider offering multilingual support or partnering with local customer service providers.

7. Currency and Payment Processing

Accommodate local currencies and payment methods to ease transactions for international users. A seamless and secure payment process encourages conversions and user retention.

8. Taxation and Invoicing

Adhere to local tax regulations for invoicing and tax collection. Tax compliance is a complex aspect of international expansion and should be addressed rigorously.

9. Data Privacy and GDPR Compliance

Ensure your data privacy policies align with international standards, especially with the General Data Protection Regulation (GDPR) in the European Union. Adherence to data protection laws is vital for user trust and to avoid potential legal consequences.

10. User Experience Testing

Testing your product's user experience in the target market is crucial. Assess how well it performs and caters to the needs and expectations of local users. Conduct usability testing and gather feedback to make necessary improvements.

11. Competitive Analysis

Understand the competitive landscape in the new market. Identify your direct and indirect competitors, their pricing strategies, and market positioning. Use this information to fine-tune your strategy and differentiate your SaaS product effectively.

12. Network and Infrastructure Considerations

Geographical distance can impact network latency and performance. Ensure your infrastructure is optimized to deliver fast and reliable service to international users. Content delivery networks (CDNs) and data centers in proximity to your users can help.

13. Marketing and Promotion

Your marketing strategy should be tailored to the target market. Focus on local SEO, social media channels, and advertising platforms to reach your potential users. Collaborate with local influencers and businesses to expand your reach.

14. International Hiring

Consider hiring local talent with knowledge of the market and culture. Local teams can provide invaluable insights and relationships that facilitate market entry and adaptation.

15. Time Zone Management

Coordinating operations and support across different time zones can be challenging. Establish a system to manage time zone differences effectively, whether through shift scheduling or 24/7 customer support availability.

16. Intellectual Property Protection

Protect your intellectual property through international patents, trademarks, and copyrights. This safeguards your SaaS product and brand identity in the target market.

17. Financial Management

International expansion requires careful financial planning. Consider currency exchange risks, international banking, and local taxation. Budget for expansion and maintain financial stability during the initial phases.

18. User Data Storage and Sovereignty

Comply with user data sovereignty laws in the target market. Users may expect their data to be stored within their country or region to ensure privacy and security.

19. Localization of Marketing Materials

Adapt marketing materials to suit the local market's preferences and culture. This includes not only language but also imagery, messaging, and references that resonate with the target audience.

20. Learning and Adaptation

International expansion is a learning process. Continuously gather feedback and adapt to the evolving needs and preferences of your international user base. Flexibility and agility are key to success in new markets.

International expansion is a complex and dynamic process. By conducting thorough research, addressing legal and regulatory considerations, and respecting local culture and user expectations, you can successfully scale your SaaS business globally. International growth opens up new possibilities for your business and can be a significant driver of long-term success.

Chapter 9: SaaS Case Studies

Success Stories from SaaS Companies

In the world of Software as a Service (SaaS), success stories inspire, educate, and offer valuable insights into the journey of SaaS companies. By exploring the experiences and achievements of established and emerging SaaS businesses, we can gain a deeper understanding of the strategies, innovations, and challenges that have shaped their paths to success. This chapter showcases a selection of SaaS case studies from diverse industries, highlighting their growth, innovation, and impact.

1. Salesforce

Industry: Customer Relationship Management (CRM)

Salesforce is a global leader in cloud-based CRM software. Founded in 1999, Salesforce revolutionized how companies manage their customer relationships. Today, it's one of the most recognizable names in the SaaS industry, with over 150,000 customers.

Key Success Factors:

- **Innovation:** Salesforce continuously introduces new features and products, staying ahead of CRM industry trends.

- **Customer-Centric Approach:** A strong focus on customer success and satisfaction has been a core principle.

- **Acquisitions:** Strategic acquisitions of companies like Tableau and MuleSoft expanded their capabilities and offerings.

2. Slack

Industry: Team Collaboration and Communication

Slack, founded in 2013, transformed workplace communication. Its platform provides teams with a centralized hub for messaging, file sharing, and collaboration.

Key Success Factors:

- **User Experience:** Slack's user-friendly interface and integration capabilities gained wide adoption among businesses.

- **Platform Ecosystem:** It encourages third-party developers to create apps, expanding its functionality.

- **Agile Development:** Slack's quick response to user feedback and feature requests kept it relevant and innovative.

3. Zoom Video Communications

Industry: Video Conferencing and Communication

Zoom, founded in 2011, redefined video conferencing by offering a high-quality, user-friendly solution. It became especially prominent during the COVID-19 pandemic.

Key Success Factors:

- **Simplicity:** Zoom's straightforward interface and ease of use made it accessible to a wide audience.

- **Reliability:** The platform's consistent performance and minimal downtime boosted its reputation.

- **Scalability:** Zoom efficiently served both individual users and large enterprises, accommodating diverse needs.

4. Shopify

Industry: E-commerce

Shopify, established in 2006, empowers entrepreneurs and businesses to create online stores and sell products. It's renowned for its flexibility and scalability.

Key Success Factors:

- **Accessibility:** Shopify's platform is user-friendly and doesn't require extensive technical knowledge to set up and manage.

- **Customization:** The ability to tailor online stores to specific brand needs attracted a diverse range of businesses.

- **Ecosystem:** Shopify's app store offers numerous integrations and tools to enhance e-commerce functionality.

5. Dropbox

Industry: File Storage and Collaboration

Dropbox, launched in 2007, simplified file storage and sharing. It quickly gained popularity for its intuitive interface and cross-platform compatibility.

Key Success Factors:

- **User Adoption:** Dropbox's straightforward design encouraged widespread adoption among individual users and businesses.

- **Cross-Platform Compatibility:** Being available on various devices and platforms made it versatile.

- **File Sharing Features:** Dropbox's sharing and collaboration features attracted a broad user base.

6. Atlassian

Industry: Team Collaboration and Productivity Tools

Atlassian, founded in 2002, is known for products like Jira, Confluence, and Trello, which help teams manage projects, track issues, and collaborate effectively.

Key Success Factors:

- **Product Portfolio:** A diverse range of products cater to various team needs, ensuring a broad customer base.

- **Developer-Friendly:** Atlassian encourages third-party app development, creating a robust ecosystem.

- **Customer-Centric Approach:** Their commitment to customer feedback and continuous improvement is a cornerstone of their success.

7. DocuSign

Industry: E-signature and Digital Transaction Management

DocuSign, established in 2003, transformed how contracts and agreements are signed. Their digital transaction management platform simplifies processes.

Key Success Factors:

- **Legally Binding:** DocuSign's platform adheres to legal standards, giving users confidence in the security of their transactions.

- **Integration Capability:** Seamless integration with other applications makes it valuable for businesses.

- **Global Reach:** The ability to serve users globally broadened their customer base.

8. Canva

Industry: Graphic Design and Publishing

Canva, founded in 2012, democratized graphic design. It offers an easy-to-use platform with templates, design tools, and stock photos.

Key Success Factors:

- **Accessibility:** Canva's simplicity allows users with no design experience to create professional-looking graphics.

- **Freemium Model:** Offering a free version with premium features drove adoption and upselling.

- **Collaboration Features:** The ability to collaborate on designs makes it attractive for teams.

9. HubSpot

Industry: Inbound Marketing and Sales Software

HubSpot, founded in 2006, provides tools for marketing, sales, and customer service. Its inbound marketing methodology has been influential.

Key Success Factors:

- **Inbound Approach:** HubSpot's focus on content marketing and inbound strategies helped it stand out in the industry.

- **All-in-One Platform:** Offering a comprehensive suite of tools simplifies marketing and sales processes.

- **Community:** HubSpot Academy and its active user community support users with resources and knowledge.

10. Zendesk

Industry: Customer Support and Service Software

Zendesk, established in 2007, offers a customer service and engagement platform that enhances customer support operations.

Key Success Factors:

- **User-Friendly:** Zendesk's interface is intuitive, making it easy for agents and customers to use.

- **Scalability:** The platform can serve both small businesses and large enterprises, offering flexibility.

- **Integration:** It integrates seamlessly with other tools, streamlining support processes.

Conclusion

These SaaS case studies offer a glimpse into the dynamic and innovative landscape of Software as a Service. From CRM giants like Salesforce to startups that disrupt industries, the SaaS industry continually evolves, driven by a commitment to user-friendly design, innovative features, and customer-centric approaches. The success stories of these companies inspire and offer valuable insights for businesses striving to make their mark in the SaaS world.

Lessons Learned from Failures

While success stories in the Software as a Service (SaaS) industry inspire and motivate, it's equally crucial to examine the lessons learned from failures. Understanding the reasons behind SaaS business failures can provide valuable insights and prevent others from making similar mistakes. In this chapter, we explore a few cautionary tales from the world of SaaS and the lessons we can extract from these experiences.

1. Quibi

Industry: Mobile Streaming

Quibi, founded in 2020, aimed to revolutionize mobile streaming with high-quality, short-form content. Despite substantial funding and star-studded content, the platform shut down just six months after its launch.

Lessons Learned:

- **Know Your Audience:** Quibi overestimated the demand for premium short-form content. Understanding your target audience and their preferences is paramount.

- **Business Model:** A subscription-based model without a free tier may not work for new entrants. Offering a free trial could attract more users.

- **Content Strategy:** The company invested heavily in content but didn't take into account that user-generated content was flourishing on platforms like TikTok. A strong content strategy should align with market trends.

2. Juicero

Industry: Food-Tech

Juicero, established in 2013, created a high-tech juicing machine that squeezed juice from pre-packaged pouches. Despite early enthusiasm and significant investments, the company ceased operations in 2017.

Lessons Learned:

- **Value Proposition:** The value of a product should be clear and practical. Juicero's machine didn't provide sufficient value over traditional juicing methods.

- **Cost Considerations:** High production and maintenance costs made the product unaffordable for many potential customers. Pricing should align with the market.

- **Market Research:** A better understanding of the market and user needs could have revealed the lack of demand for an expensive juicing machine.

3. MoviePass

Industry: Movie Subscription Services

MoviePass, launched in 2011, allowed users to watch multiple movies in theaters for a low monthly fee. The service rapidly gained users but ran into financial and operational challenges.

Lessons Learned:

- **Sustainable Pricing:** MoviePass's pricing model was unsustainable. Offering unlimited movies at a low price without considering the cost of tickets was a critical mistake.

- **Cash Flow Management:** Poor cash flow management and uncontrolled expenses led to financial difficulties. A clear financial strategy is essential.

- **Customer Communication:** Frequent changes to the service without clear communication frustrated users. Consistent and transparent communication is vital.

4. Color Labs

Industry: Photo Sharing and Social Media

Color Labs, founded in 2010, aimed to create a new social media platform for photo sharing. Despite significant initial funding, the company failed to gain traction.

Lessons Learned:

- **Market Fit:** A new social media platform should address unmet needs or offer unique features. Color Labs failed to differentiate itself in a crowded space.

- **User Onboarding:** The user experience was complicated, making it difficult for users to understand the value of the platform. A user-friendly interface is essential.

- **Monetization Strategy:** The company struggled to establish a clear monetization strategy. Understanding how the platform will generate revenue is crucial.

5. Rdio

Industry: Music Streaming

Rdio, launched in 2010, was an early entrant in the music streaming industry. Despite critical acclaim for its user interface and design, it couldn't compete with giants like Spotify.

Lessons Learned:

- **Market Timing:** Entering a market with entrenched competitors requires a strong differentiator. Rdio couldn't offer enough to convince users to switch from established platforms.

- **Licensing Costs:** Music streaming services face significant licensing costs. Understanding the financial implications and negotiating favorable deals are vital.

- **User Acquisition:** Rdio struggled with user acquisition and retention. Effective marketing and user engagement strategies are critical.

6. Blippar

Industry: Augmented Reality (AR) and Visual Search

Blippar, established in 2011, aimed to bring AR and visual search to everyday life. Despite early enthusiasm and innovative technology, the company faced financial troubles.

Lessons Learned:

- **Monetization Model:** Blippar's technology was innovative, but it struggled to find a sustainable monetization model. Identifying revenue sources early is crucial.

- **Market Adoption:** AR and visual search faced slow adoption, and Blippar failed to bridge the gap effectively. Understanding market dynamics and user behavior is vital.

- **Competitive Landscape:** The company faced competition from tech giants like Google, making it challenging to establish a foothold. Assessing the competitive landscape is essential.

7. Jawbone

Industry: Wearable Technology and Fitness Tracking

Jawbone, founded in 1999, was an early player in wearable fitness technology. Despite initial success, the company faced financial issues and legal disputes.

Lessons Learned:

- **Product Quality:** Jawbone's products faced quality issues and frequent recalls, damaging its reputation. Consistently delivering quality products is crucial.

- **Market Evolution:** The wearable technology market evolved rapidly, and Jawbone couldn't keep up with changing trends. Adaptability and innovation are essential.

- **Legal Challenges:** Legal disputes can be costly and disruptive. Avoiding or effectively addressing legal issues is vital.

8. Secret

Industry: Social Networking and Anonymous Sharing

Secret, launched in 2014, allowed users to share secrets anonymously with their contacts. Despite initial buzz, the platform faced challenges and ceased operations in 2015.

Lessons Learned:

- **User Safety:** Anonymous sharing can lead to cyberbullying and other safety concerns. Ensuring a safe user experience is essential.

- **Monetization Strategy:** The company struggled to establish a clear monetization strategy. Understanding how the platform will generate revenue is crucial.

- **Market Fit:** Secret couldn't establish a strong market fit, and user engagement declined. Understanding user needs is essential.

The SaaS industry is replete with stories of both success and failure. While success stories inspire and provide valuable insights, learning from the failures of others is equally crucial. The lessons from these SaaS case studies illustrate the importance of understanding market dynamics, user needs, sustainable business models, and effective communication. Examining these cautionary tales can help SaaS businesses navigate the challenges and pitfalls that come their way, ultimately leading to a higher likelihood of success.

Innovation in SaaS

The Software as a Service (SaaS) industry is a hotbed of innovation, where companies continually push the boundaries of technology to deliver new solutions and enhance existing ones. In this chapter, we delve into a selection of SaaS case studies that exemplify the spirit of innovation, exploring how these companies have harnessed creativity, technology, and customer-centricity to drive progress and shape the future of SaaS.

1. Slack

Industry: Team Collaboration and Communication

Slack is a prime example of how innovation can transform the way teams collaborate and communicate. Launched in 2013, Slack quickly disrupted the traditional email-based workplace communication. Its user-friendly interface and integrations have made it a hub for real-time messaging, file sharing, and collaboration, with over 12 million daily active users as of 2019.

Innovative Aspects:

- **Integration Ecosystem:** Slack's success hinges on its ability to integrate with a wide array of third-party applications. This ecosystem allows users to seamlessly connect and collaborate within their preferred tools, creating an environment conducive to productivity.

- **User Experience:** The platform's focus on an intuitive and enjoyable user experience sets it apart. Slack's emphasis on user feedback and continuous improvement is a testament to its commitment to innovation.

- **Channels and Customization:** Slack introduced the concept of channels, enabling teams to organize conversations by topic. Users can also customize the platform with apps and bots, tailoring it to their specific needs.

2. Zoom Video Communications

Industry: Video Conferencing and Communication

Zoom, founded in 2011, represents a transformative force in the world of video conferencing. The platform's innovative approach to virtual meetings has made it a household name, especially during the COVID-19 pandemic when remote work and virtual meetings became the norm.

Innovative Aspects:

- **Quality and Reliability:** Zoom's commitment to delivering high-quality video and audio, along with minimal downtime, has been instrumental in its success. Innovations in compression algorithms and data optimization contribute to a seamless experience.

- **Ease of Use:** Zoom's straightforward design and user-friendly interface allow participants to join meetings with minimal effort. This focus on simplicity has fueled its widespread adoption.

- **Scalability:** Zoom serves both individual users and large enterprises with ease, accommodating diverse needs. The platform's scalability is a key aspect of its innovation.

3. Shopify

Industry: E-commerce

Shopify, established in 2006, has redefined e-commerce with its innovative platform. By empowering entrepreneurs and businesses to create their online stores and sell products, Shopify has democratized online commerce.

Innovative Aspects:

- **Accessibility:** Shopify's user-friendly platform doesn't require extensive technical knowledge, making it accessible to a broad audience. The democratization of e-commerce is central to its innovation.

- **Customization:** Shopify's flexibility allows businesses to tailor their online stores to specific brand needs. This customization empowers businesses to stand out in a crowded marketplace.

- **Ecosystem:** Shopify's app store offers a wide range of integrations and tools to enhance e-commerce functionality. This ecosystem of third-party apps adds a layer of innovation to the platform.

4. Canva

Industry: Graphic Design and Publishing

Canva, founded in 2012, has made graphic design accessible to everyone. With an innovative platform that offers templates, design tools, and a vast library of stock photos, Canva has transformed the way individuals and businesses create visual content.

Innovative Aspects:

- **Accessibility:** Canva's intuitive and user-friendly platform allows users with no design experience to create professional-looking graphics. The democratization of design is at the core of its innovation.

- **Freemium Model:** Offering a free version with premium features has driven user adoption and upselling. The freemium model is an innovative approach to pricing.

- **Collaboration Features:** Canva enables users to collaborate on designs, fostering teamwork and innovation in the design process.

5. HubSpot

Industry: Inbound Marketing and Sales Software

HubSpot, founded in 2006, is a pioneer in the world of inbound marketing. Its innovative approach to content marketing and sales strategies has made it a leader in the field.

Innovative Aspects:

- **Inbound Methodology:** HubSpot's emphasis on inbound marketing and content creation has transformed the way businesses attract and engage customers. This methodology has been a revolutionary force in the industry.

- **All-in-One Platform:** Offering a comprehensive suite of marketing, sales, and customer service tools in one platform simplifies processes and fosters innovation within businesses.

- **Community and Education:** HubSpot Academy and its active user community provide resources and knowledge that empower users to innovate in their marketing and sales efforts.

6. Zendesk

Industry: Customer Support and Service Software

Zendesk, established in 2007, has been an innovative force in the field of customer support and service software. Its user-friendly platform simplifies customer service operations and fosters innovation in support delivery.

Innovative Aspects:

- **User-Centric Design:** Zendesk's user-friendly interface allows both agents and customers to interact seamlessly. This focus on user experience promotes innovation in support delivery.

- **Scalability:** Zendesk efficiently serves both small businesses and large enterprises, demonstrating the platform's adaptability and innovation in addressing diverse customer needs.

- **Integration Capabilities:** Zendesk integrates seamlessly with other tools, streamlining support processes and fostering innovation in customer service delivery.

Innovation is the very important in the SaaS industry. The case studies of Slack, Zoom, Shopify, Canva, HubSpot, and Zendesk demonstrate that SaaS companies thrive by embracing innovation. Whether through creating user-friendly platforms, fostering ecosystems of third-party integrations, democratizing design and commerce, or pioneering new approaches to marketing and customer service, these companies have transformed their respective industries. Their success stories serve as inspiration and a reminder that innovation remains at the heart of SaaS evolution.

Chapter 10: The Future of SaaS

Emerging Trends in SaaS

As technology and customer needs change, SaaS companies must adapt and innovate to stay relevant. In this chapter, we explore some of the most significant emerging trends in the world of SaaS, offering a glimpse into the future of the industry.

1. Artificial Intelligence and Machine Learning Integration

Artificial intelligence (AI) and machine learning (ML) are poised to revolutionize SaaS applications. These technologies enable SaaS platforms to deliver smarter, more personalized services. AI and ML can enhance user experiences by predicting user behavior, automating tasks, and providing data-driven insights.

- *Example:* Customer relationship management (CRM) software integrated with AI can analyze customer interactions to identify potential leads and recommend personalized marketing strategies.

2. Multi-Cloud Strategies

Multi-cloud strategies involve using multiple cloud providers to ensure redundancy, flexibility, and enhanced performance. SaaS providers are increasingly adopting multi-cloud architectures to avoid vendor lock-in, improve reliability, and offer customers the freedom to choose their preferred cloud platform.

- *Example:* A SaaS platform might use both AWS and Microsoft Azure to diversify its cloud infrastructure, providing customers with options for where their data is hosted.

3. Edge Computing for SaaS

Edge computing brings computing power closer to the data source, reducing latency and enabling real-time data processing. SaaS providers are adopting edge computing to offer faster and more responsive services, particularly in applications where immediate data processing is critical.

- *Example:* SaaS applications for autonomous vehicles leverage edge computing to process sensor data on-board, ensuring rapid decision-making.

4. Blockchain for Data Security and Transparency

Blockchain technology offers enhanced security, transparency, and data integrity. SaaS platforms are exploring the integration of blockchain for applications such as data encryption, secure sharing, and smart contracts, ensuring trust and security in data transactions.

- *Example:* Supply chain management SaaS solutions use blockchain to create an immutable ledger of product movements, enhancing transparency and traceability.

5. Serverless Computing

Serverless computing, also known as Function as a Service (FaaS), abstracts server management from application development. SaaS providers are adopting serverless architectures to enhance scalability, reduce operational overhead, and focus on building innovative features.

- *Example:* SaaS platforms use serverless functions to automatically scale resources based on demand, providing cost-effective and efficient services.

6. Quantum Computing Applications

Quantum computing is still in its early stages, but its potential for breaking traditional encryption and solving complex problems could impact SaaS. While full-scale quantum computing is a future prospect, SaaS companies are already exploring how to secure data in a quantum-ready world.

- *Example:* SaaS providers are researching post-quantum cryptography to ensure data security in a quantum computing era.

7. No-Code and Low-Code Platforms

No-code and low-code development platforms empower non-developers to create software applications without writing extensive code. SaaS companies are integrating these platforms to accelerate application development and democratize the creation of custom applications.

- *Example:* A SaaS provider might offer a low-code interface for customers to build tailored workflows within their application.

8. Sustainability and Eco-Friendly Practices

Environmental concerns are driving SaaS companies to adopt more sustainable practices. From data center efficiency to reducing carbon footprints, sustainability is becoming a key focus area. SaaS providers are increasingly investing in renewable energy, efficient data centers, and carbon offset programs.

- *Example:* SaaS companies may commit to using 100% renewable energy to power their data centers, reducing their carbon emissions.

9. Augmented Reality (AR) and Virtual Reality (VR) Integration

AR and VR technologies are expanding beyond gaming and entertainment, finding applications in SaaS. These immersive technologies offer new ways to interact with data, conduct training, and visualize complex information.

- *Example:* SaaS providers for architecture and interior design use VR to allow clients to experience virtual walkthroughs of spaces.

10. Enhanced Data Privacy and Security

As data breaches and privacy concerns become more prevalent, SaaS providers are focusing on enhancing data privacy and security measures. This includes robust encryption, advanced authentication, and compliance with evolving data protection regulations.

- *Example:* SaaS platforms implement end-to-end encryption to secure user data, ensuring that even service providers can't access sensitive information.

11. Personalized Customer Experiences

SaaS platforms are increasingly focused on personalization to improve customer satisfaction and retention. By leveraging AI and data analytics, SaaS providers can offer tailored experiences, from content recommendations to user interfaces.

- *Example:* SaaS applications use machine learning algorithms to analyze user behavior and provide personalized content and features.

12. 5G Network Adoption

The rollout of 5G networks has significant implications for SaaS. The increased speed and low latency offered by 5G enable more real-time and bandwidth-intensive SaaS applications, expanding the possibilities for cloud-based services.

- *Example:* Streaming services and cloud-based gaming platforms can leverage 5G to provide smoother and higher-quality experiences.

13. Globalization and Localization

As SaaS platforms expand globally, localization becomes essential. This includes adapting to regional regulations, languages, and cultural nuances, allowing SaaS providers to serve a diverse international customer base effectively.

- *Example:* SaaS providers might offer user interfaces and customer support in multiple languages, ensuring accessibility for users worldwide.

14. Ethical AI and Bias Mitigation

Ethical considerations surrounding AI and machine learning are becoming paramount. SaaS companies are focusing on mitigating bias, ensuring fairness, and maintaining ethical AI practices in their solutions.

- *Example:* SaaS providers employ AI auditing tools to assess and mitigate potential biases in their algorithms, promoting fairness and transparency.

15. Remote Work Tools

The shift to remote work has driven the development of innovative SaaS tools that support remote collaboration, project management, and communication. As remote work becomes a permanent feature of the modern workplace, these tools continue to evolve.

- *Example:* SaaS providers offer virtual whiteboards, advanced video conferencing, and team collaboration platforms designed for remote work.

16. Sustainable Software Development

SaaS providers are increasingly adopting sustainable software development practices, aiming to reduce the environmental impact of software creation. This includes optimizing code for energy efficiency and reducing resource consumption.

- *Example:* SaaS companies assess the environmental footprint of their software development processes and implement strategies to minimize energy consumption.

The future of SaaS is a landscape of ongoing innovation and adaptation. As technology evolves and customer needs change, SaaS providers are at the forefront of delivering cutting-edge solutions. Whether through the integration of AI, blockchain, or quantum computing, SaaS is poised to revolutionize industries and improve the lives of individuals and businesses worldwide. By embracing emerging trends and staying ahead of the curve, SaaS companies will continue to shape the future of software delivery.

AI and Machine Learning in SaaS

The SaaS industry is on the cusp of a technological revolution driven by the integration of Artificial Intelligence (AI) and Machine Learning (ML). These transformative technologies are reshaping how SaaS platforms operate, offering unprecedented capabilities that enhance user experiences, drive efficiency, and open doors to new possibilities. In this chapter, we explore the significant impact of AI and ML in the future of SaaS.

1. Enhanced Personalization

AI and ML algorithms empower SaaS platforms to deliver highly personalized experiences. By analyzing user behavior and preferences, SaaS applications can provide tailored content, recommendations, and features. This level of personalization not only increases user engagement but also fosters customer loyalty.

Example: A streaming service utilizes ML to analyze user viewing habits and provides custom-tailored movie recommendations, improving the user's experience.

2. Predictive Analytics

AI and ML enable SaaS platforms to harness the power of predictive analytics. These technologies can anticipate user needs, trends, and potential issues, allowing SaaS providers to proactively address challenges and offer valuable insights.

Example: A marketing automation SaaS predicts customer churn based on user interactions, helping businesses implement retention strategies.

3. Automation of Repetitive Tasks

AI and ML are streamlining processes by automating repetitive and time-consuming tasks. SaaS platforms leverage these technologies to handle data entry, document processing, and other routine operations, saving users time and reducing errors.

Example: A project management SaaS uses AI to automate task assignment, prioritization, and tracking, enhancing team efficiency.

4. Natural Language Processing (NLP)

NLP is a subset of AI that enables SaaS platforms to understand and respond to human language. Chatbots and virtual assistants integrated into SaaS applications can interact with users, answer queries, and provide assistance, improving user engagement and support.

Example: An e-commerce SaaS employs a chatbot that uses NLP to answer customer questions, offer product recommendations, and assist with purchases.

5. Data-Driven Decision Making

AI and ML facilitate data-driven decision making by extracting valuable insights from large datasets. SaaS providers can offer data analytics tools that allow users to make informed decisions based on the analysis of vast amounts of information.

Example: A financial SaaS provides AI-powered data analytics, enabling users to assess market trends and make investment decisions with greater confidence.

6. Improved Cybersecurity

AI and ML play a crucial role in enhancing cybersecurity within SaaS applications. These technologies can detect and respond to security threats in real-time, helping SaaS platforms protect user data and maintain robust security measures.

Example: An email security SaaS employs ML to detect phishing attempts, malicious attachments, and suspicious activity, safeguarding users from cyber threats.

7. Sentiment Analysis

AI-driven sentiment analysis can gauge public opinion, user feedback, and social media chatter. SaaS platforms can utilize this technology to understand user sentiment, monitor brand reputation, and make data-driven adjustments.

Example: A social media management SaaS utilizes sentiment analysis to track user comments, assess customer satisfaction, and adjust marketing strategies accordingly.

8. Content Generation

AI and ML have advanced to the point where they can generate content such as reports, articles, and even creative works. SaaS platforms can leverage this technology to automate content creation, saving users time and effort.

Example: A content marketing SaaS uses AI to generate blog posts based on user-provided keywords and topics, streamlining content creation.

9. Advanced Search and Discovery

AI-powered search and discovery features enhance the user experience within SaaS applications. These technologies can understand user intent, improve search results, and offer relevant suggestions.

Example: An e-commerce SaaS employs AI to enhance product search, providing more accurate results and suggesting related items.

10. Continuous Learning and Adaptation

AI and ML models continuously learn and adapt to changing circumstances. SaaS platforms can take advantage of this capability to stay updated with user preferences, market trends, and evolving requirements.

Example: An e-learning SaaS uses ML to adapt course materials and difficulty levels based on individual student progress, ensuring optimal learning outcomes.

11. Improved User Support

AI-driven chatbots and virtual assistants offer immediate and round-the-clock support to SaaS users. These bots can answer frequently asked questions, guide users through troubleshooting, and provide assistance, reducing the burden on customer support teams.

Example: A customer service SaaS integrates an AI chatbot to handle common support inquiries, providing quicker responses to users.

12. Fraud Detection and Prevention

AI and ML play a critical role in fraud detection and prevention within SaaS applications. These technologies can analyze transaction data, identify anomalies, and flag potential fraudulent activities.

Example: An e-commerce payment processing SaaS employs ML to detect irregular transaction patterns, helping prevent fraudulent payments.

13. Augmented Reality (AR) and Virtual Reality (VR) Integration

AI and ML are instrumental in AR and VR technologies, enabling immersive experiences within SaaS applications. These technologies offer new ways to visualize data, conduct training, and enhance user engagement.

Example: A real estate SaaS integrates VR to offer virtual property tours, allowing clients to explore listings from the comfort of their homes.

14. Sustainable Practices

AI and ML can be used to optimize SaaS operations for sustainability. By analyzing energy usage and resource consumption, SaaS providers can reduce their environmental footprint, contributing to eco-friendly practices.

Example: A data center management SaaS employs AI to monitor and manage energy consumption, reducing the environmental impact of server operations.

15. Ethical AI and Bias Mitigation

AI and ML are adopting ethical principles to mitigate bias and ensure fairness. SaaS providers are increasingly committed to implementing responsible AI practices and preventing discrimination in their algorithms.

Example: A hiring and recruitment SaaS employs bias detection algorithms to ensure fairness and diversity in the selection process.

Conclusion

AI and Machine Learning are driving the future of SaaS, revolutionizing the capabilities and opportunities available to users and businesses. These technologies empower SaaS platforms to deliver enhanced personalization, predictive analytics, automation, NLP, and much more. With AI and ML as cornerstones, SaaS is evolving to meet the ever-changing needs of its users, fostering innovation, and delivering transformative solutions across industries. The future of SaaS is an exciting landscape shaped by intelligence and adaptability, where possibilities are limited only by the imagination.

The Impact of SaaS on Other Industries

The SaaS industry has not only transformed the software delivery model but has also had a profound impact on a wide range of other industries. As SaaS applications continue to evolve and expand, their influence extends beyond the realm of software. In this chapter, we explore how SaaS is shaping and revolutionizing various sectors, from healthcare to education, and beyond.

1. Healthcare and Telemedicine

The healthcare industry has seen a significant transformation thanks to SaaS applications. Electronic Health Records (EHRs), telemedicine platforms, and health management systems have become critical in providing better patient care and streamlining healthcare operations.

Example: Telemedicine SaaS platforms enable patients to connect with healthcare providers remotely, improving access to medical services and reducing the need for in-person visits.

2. Education and E-Learning

The education sector has embraced SaaS applications to enhance teaching, learning, and administrative tasks. Learning Management Systems (LMS), online courses, and virtual classrooms have become essential tools for educators and students.

Example: Educational institutions use LMS SaaS platforms to deliver course materials, track student progress, and facilitate online discussions, making learning more accessible and flexible.

3. Financial Services and Fintech

The financial industry has been disrupted by SaaS applications, particularly in the field of financial technology (fintech). From online banking to budgeting and investment platforms, SaaS solutions are changing how people manage and invest their money.

Example: Fintech SaaS platforms provide users with real-time financial data, budgeting tools, and investment advice, empowering individuals to make informed financial decisions.

4. Retail and E-Commerce

The retail industry has adopted SaaS solutions for e-commerce, inventory management, and customer relationship management. These applications enable retailers to reach a global audience, streamline operations, and improve customer experiences.

Example: E-commerce SaaS platforms offer features like online storefronts, shopping carts, and secure payment processing, making it easier for businesses to sell products online.

5. Manufacturing and Supply Chain

SaaS applications have revolutionized the manufacturing and supply chain sectors. These solutions provide real-time insights into inventory, production, and logistics, allowing companies to optimize processes and reduce costs.

Example: Supply chain SaaS platforms offer end-to-end visibility into the movement of goods, helping businesses make informed decisions to improve efficiency and reduce waste.

6. Real Estate and Property Management

Real estate professionals and property managers use SaaS applications to streamline property management, listings, and tenant communication. These tools enhance the property rental and sales process.

Example: Property management SaaS platforms assist landlords in tenant screening, rent collection, and property maintenance, simplifying property management tasks.

7. Legal and Compliance

Legal professionals and organizations leverage SaaS applications for legal research, document management, and compliance tracking. These solutions streamline legal processes and improve access to legal information.

Example: Legal research SaaS platforms provide attorneys with an extensive database of legal documents and precedents, facilitating research and case preparation.

8. Human Resources and Talent Management

The HR industry relies on SaaS applications for various tasks, including recruitment, onboarding, payroll, and employee management. These platforms simplify HR processes and enhance employee engagement.

Example: HR SaaS platforms offer features like applicant tracking, performance management, and benefits administration, making it easier for companies to manage their workforce.

9. Marketing and Advertising

The marketing and advertising industry has seen a transformation with the advent of SaaS applications. These platforms offer tools for email marketing, social media management, data analytics, and ad campaign tracking.

Example: Marketing automation SaaS platforms enable businesses to automate marketing campaigns, track customer interactions, and personalize marketing efforts.

10. Construction and Project Management

The construction and project management sector benefits from SaaS solutions that enhance project planning, collaboration, and cost management. These applications enable construction companies to complete projects more efficiently.

Example: Construction project management SaaS platforms facilitate project scheduling, document sharing, and communication among project stakeholders, improving project outcomes.

11. Environmental and Sustainability

SaaS applications are making significant contributions to environmental sustainability. They help organizations track and reduce their environmental impact by providing tools for energy efficiency, waste reduction, and sustainability reporting.

Example: Environmental sustainability SaaS platforms offer tools to monitor energy usage, reduce waste, and calculate an organization's carbon footprint, contributing to eco-friendly practices.

12. Travel and Hospitality

The travel and hospitality industry relies on SaaS applications for booking, reservations, customer management, and loyalty programs. These platforms enhance the traveler's experience and improve business operations.

Example: Hotel management SaaS platforms assist with online bookings, room assignments, and guest services, offering a seamless experience for both guests and staff.

13. Agriculture and Agtech

The agricultural sector is embracing SaaS solutions to improve crop management, yield prediction, and resource utilization. These applications enhance agricultural practices, reduce waste, and boost yields.

Example: Agtech SaaS platforms provide farmers with data on weather, soil conditions, and crop health, allowing for precise resource allocation and improved harvests.

14. Nonprofits and Fundraising

Nonprofit organizations rely on SaaS applications for donor management, online fundraising, and campaign tracking. These platforms help nonprofits reach a broader audience and raise funds more efficiently.

Example: Nonprofit fundraising SaaS platforms offer online donation processing, donor engagement, and campaign analytics, simplifying the fundraising process.

15. Government and Public Services

Government agencies utilize SaaS applications for citizen engagement, document management, and administrative tasks. These solutions enhance government services, increase transparency, and improve citizen interactions.

Example: Government SaaS platforms offer citizens online services such as permit applications, tax filings, and public records access, making government services more accessible.

16. Energy and Utilities

The energy and utilities industry leverages SaaS applications for energy monitoring, grid management, and customer service. These platforms help utilities improve service delivery and grid efficiency.

Example: Utility management SaaS platforms provide utilities with real-time data on energy usage, grid performance, and customer billing, enhancing service quality.

17. Entertainment and Streaming Services

SaaS applications are central to the entertainment and streaming industry. They enable content delivery, user management, and content recommendation, creating immersive and personalized entertainment experiences.

Example: Video streaming SaaS platforms offer on-demand content, personalized recommendations, and multi-device access, enhancing the viewer's experience.

18. Sports and Fitness

The sports and fitness industry has embraced SaaS solutions for fitness tracking, coaching, and fan engagement. These platforms enable athletes, coaches, and fans to stay connected and informed.

Example: Fitness tracking SaaS platforms provide users with workout routines, progress tracking, and nutritional advice, helping individuals achieve their fitness goals.

19. Transportation and Mobility

The transportation and mobility sector uses SaaS applications for ride-sharing, navigation, and logistics management. These platforms improve transportation efficiency and traveler experiences.

Example: Ride-sharing SaaS platforms connect drivers and passengers, offering real-time route planning, cost estimation, and secure payments, simplifying travel.

20. Non-SaaS Industries

Even in industries not traditionally associated with SaaS, organizations are finding ways to leverage SaaS applications to streamline operations and enhance customer experiences.

Example: Restaurants and food services may employ SaaS solutions for online ordering, reservation management, and customer loyalty programs, improving dining experiences.

21. The SaaS Ecosystem

The SaaS ecosystem itself has expanded, fostering collaboration and innovation across industries. SaaS marketplaces, integrations, and API ecosystems allow businesses to build custom solutions tailored to their unique needs.

Example: Businesses in various industries leverage SaaS integrations to connect their CRM, marketing, and customer support platforms, creating a seamless customer journey.

Conclusion

The impact of SaaS on other industries is undeniable. SaaS applications have transcended the boundaries of traditional software delivery, reshaping how various sectors operate and providing opportunities for innovation and growth. From healthcare and education to finance, agriculture, and beyond, SaaS continues to revolutionize and drive efficiency in diverse industries. As SaaS applications evolve, they will undoubtedly play an even more significant role in shaping the future of these sectors.

SaaS

www.ingramcontent.com/pod-product-compliance
Lightning Source LLC
Chambersburg PA
CBHW062321290526
45794CB00005B/1847